Contents

Illustrations

All illustrations are from the author's collection.

Get Carter

STEVE CHIBNALL

I.B. TAURIS
LONDON · NEW YORK

Published in 2003 by I.B.Tauris & Co. Ltd
6 Salem Road, London W2 4BU
175 Fifth Avenue, New York NY 10010
www.ibtauris.com

In the United States of America and Canada distributed by Palgrave
Macmillan, a division of St Martin's Press, 175 Fifth Avenue, New York
NY 10010

ISBN 1 86064 910 6

A full CIP record for this book is available from the British Library
A full CIP record for this book is available from the Library of Congress

Library of Congress catalog card: available

Set in Monotype Fournier and Univers Black by Ewan Smith, London
Printed and bound in Great Britain by MPG Books, Bodmin

Acknowledgements

Sincere thanks are due to a number of friends in the North. Chris Riley of the *Get Carter* Appreciation Society put me on the track of call sheets and movement orders for the film, and Dave Watson of the Northern Screen Commission kindly made copies of these rare documents available to me. Amy Redpath allowed me to draw on research undertaken for her BA dissertation at De Montfort University, and Alan Burton gave me access to his interview with cinematographer Wolfgang Suschitzky. Michael Brady's remarkable website inspired me to take the *Get Carter* locations trail, and Dorothy Malone at Dryderdale Hall supplied opulent accommodation and fascinating conversation. As well as a constant source of support and encouragement, my partner, Kara McKechnie, was a wonderful travelling companion and patiently indulged my need to find the exact spots on the chilly beach at Blackhall where Eric and Jack met their maker (sad, eh?).

I must also acknowledge my series editor Jeffrey Richards and commissioning editor Philippa Brewster for making this book possible, and give a special thank you to Mike Hodges, who answered my questions with good humour and made time to read through my manuscript and check it for factual errors. This was no easy task more than thirty years after making the film, and should any errors have crept through, these are mine rather than Mike's.

This book is dedicated to the memory of the late Ted Lewis and a condemned car park in Gateshead.

Foreword

Asked to read the manuscript of this book, I was astonished by the amount of detailed research that has gone into it. Much of what the author has uncovered is 'news' to me – and would have been when I was making it – but then I made the film flying by the seat of my pants, driven by some sort of intuitive white heat. From being sent the novel, *Jack's Return Home*, to finishing the cut film took just forty weeks.

It is salutary to be reminded of the process of creativity. For film makers of my age influences have often become obscured. Ghosts in the machine. Pentimento. A film seen just once in the distant past – and I mean just 'once' – for this was long before videos. Then you will come across it decades later – usually on TV – and recognise where some 'moment' in one of your films has come from. It is always startling – fact and fiction occupying the same territory in one's brain – recognising our amazing ability to collect and store slivers of time. With that comes the realisation that originality is not quite what it seems.

Until I read this book I was never conscious of the influence of American 'westerns' on my films. I had forgotten that, alongside musicals, they were my staple diet when I was a young man – not surprising for an articled pupil bored out of his mind in a small-town accountant's office – but I have not seen one since the late 1950s. Not even on TV. I simply grew out of them – as I did musicals. I suspect this went hand in hand with my growing disillusionment with America. Yet they are undoubtedly in the compost of my life – and it seems they will out.

I am flattered that the film gets such considered attention in this book, and grateful I matured before the advent of videos. They make it even harder to be original.

Mike Hodges
Dorset, August 2002

Film Credits

UK première	10 March 1971
US première	18 March 1971

CAST

Michael Caine	Jack Carter
Ian Hendry	Eric Paice
Britt Ekland	Anna Fletcher
John Osborne	Cyril Kinnear
Tony Beckley	Peter
George Sewell	Con McCarty
Geraldine Moffat	Glenda
Dorothy White	Margaret
Rosemarie Dunham	Edna
Petra Markham	Doreen
Alun Armstrong	Keith
Bryan Mosley	Cliff Brumby
Glynn Edwards	Albert Swift
Bernard Hepton	Thorpe
Terence Rigby	Gerald Fletcher
John Bindon	Sid Fletcher
Godfrey Quigley	Eddie
Kevin Brennan	Harry
Maxwell Dees	Vicar
Liz McKenzie	Mrs Brumby
John Hussey	Architect
Ben Aris	Architect
Kitty Atwood	Old woman
Denea Wilde	Pub singer
Geraldine Sherman	Girl in cafe
Joy Merlin	Woman in post office
Yvonne Michaels	Woman in post office
Alan Hockey	Scrapyard dealer
Carl Howard	'J'
John Cavanagh	Barman (Long Bar) (uncredited)
Reg Niven	Frank Carter (dead) (uncredited)
Tracey Star	Woman in bar fight (uncredited)

ONE
Carter in Context

FROM CULT TO CLASSIC

... So shall you hear
Of carnal, bloody, and unnatural acts;
Of accidental judgments, casual slaughters;
Of deaths put on by cunning and forc'd cause;
And, in this upshot, purposes mistook
Falle'n on th' inventors' heads – all this can I
Truly deliver.

Horatio in William Shakespeare, *Hamlet* (c. 1601), v.ii.372–8

Some truths can be held to be self-evident: bears defecate in forested areas; the Pope is uncircumcised; *Get Carter* (1971) is the finest British crime film ever made. Hold on: some truths take longer than others to become self-evident. It took almost twenty-five years for the critical orthodoxy to accept that the cult followers of Mike Hodges' dark and downbeat tale of fear and loathing in Newcastle had some justification for their reverence. Clearly, the film had not changed, but something in the culture of its reception most certainly had. When Hodges spoke about his film at a screening at the National Film Theatre on 23 September 1997, he indicated that he had come to regard making a film as 'putting a message in a bottle', packing it with meaning and waiting for it to be washed up on some receptive shore.[1] By the turn of the millennium, *Get Carter* was basking on the beach. This book will play the beachcomber. It will pick up the bottle, examine its contents and wonder about its origins. But it will also be interested in the beach and the tides that deposit its celluloid flotsam and jetsam.

In her 1985 essay on the politics of film canons, Janet Staiger pointed to a developing strand of film studies that questioned the idea of a single 'correct' interpretation of any text, and 'concentrated instead on how institutions and ideologies have established appropriate methods of understanding a work'. This involved, she suggested, an analysis of 'a politics that marginalises and devalues non-elite reading strategies'.[2] Staiger's concerns with reading communities, interpretive strategies and the politics of admission to institutional canons were never more relevant than in the case of *Get Carter*, a film that has undergone a transformation from underground cult to overground classic. Staiger likened institutional anxieties about the dissolution or dilution of the film canon to the fears expressed in Umberto Eco's *The Name of the Rose* about 'dwarfs with huge bellies and immense heads' taking charge of the monastic library.[3] Well, if the critical rehabilitation of *Get Carter* is anything to go by, the British Film Institute has recently become populated by rotund people of small stature. Its millennial poll of the great and the good of British cinema placed *Carter* among the top twenty treasures of the nation's cinematic heritage.

If *Get Carter*'s place among the pantheon of British cinema classics has only recently been established, its status as a cult movie has long been unquestionable. Anyone in doubt should visit the sumptuous Web site (www.btinternet.com/~ms.dear) that devotee Mark Dear operates as a shrine for the film's fans. Replete with poster reproductions from all over the world, rare stills, accounts of the film's shooting and critical reception, chat room, and prize awards for the winners of its trivia quiz, the site speaks eloquently of the enthusiasm of generations of *Get Carter* adherents. This enthusiasm is not confined to the manipulation of a computer mouse. The *Get Carter* Appreciation Society marked the thirtieth anniversary of the film's location shooting by re-enacting various scenes in Newcastle and Gateshead on 28 July 2000. Organised by Chris Riley, a Tyneside solicitor, the event centred on the decaying Owen Luder-designed car park on the corner of West and Ellison Streets in Gateshead, the scene of Carter's murder of the 'big man' in 'bad shape', Cliff Brumby (Bryan Mosley). The car park had become 'a monument to the film', said Riley, but was targeted for demolition to make way for new developments in the town. Now fully conversant with its cultural responsibilities, Gateshead Town Centre Regeneration announced plans to present the man who played Carter, Michael Caine, with a piece of concrete from the site once the bulldozers have done their work. A spokesman for the organisation acknowledged the solemnity of the occasion when he told the press on 3 August, '*Get Carter* was a great movie and there is a lot of affection for that car park.' The growing significance of the film to a sense of local identity was acknowledged in January 2002 when Newcastle radio station Century FM dedicated a day to *Get Carter*, asking listeners to phone in with their memories of the making of the movie.

Ultimately, cult movies are defined by their appropriation by active audiences, but films do not have an equal chance of being appropriated. Commentators have frequently noted that certain textual characteristics offer greater possibilities for cultish adoption than others. Movies that acquire a cult following are often challenging and confrontational in their style, imagery and themes. They will usually transgress genre boundaries, exhibiting an 'unhinged' quality, which revels in excess. Their narratives are likely to offer scope for metaphorical or allegorical interpretation, and may resonate with deep-seated cultural myths. More often than not, they will be highly self-aware, containing coded references and intertextual allusions that allow opportunities for detective work. Frequently, too, the cult film will feature a charismatic protagonist or antagonist who becomes an unconventional object of identification for viewers, provoking ambivalent feelings in the process.[4] None of these characteristics is sufficient in itself to guarantee cult status, but the accumulation of these textual aspects will increase a film's chances of adoption. *Get Carter* is a perfect example.

CARTER AS TRAGEDY

'Tragedy is born in the west each time that the pendulum of civilization is halfway between a sacred society and a society built around man.' Albert Camus, *Selected Essays and Notebooks*, Harmondsworth: Penguin, 1970, p. 199

Get Carter is a film about crooks and, therefore, easily classified as a gangster or crime film. Its narrative of a murder solved by a lone investigator in a city rife with corrupt practices links it to the hardboiled private eye fiction of Chandler and Hammett, and its nihilistic tone, amoral atmosphere and *mise-en-scène* of urban decay recall American film noir. Commentators have also sometimes noted *Get Carter*'s affinity to the western, and there are indeed close parallels in the film's narrative structure, mood of sombre determination, and emphasis on violent individualism.[5] Its closest western genre antecedents are the personal justice sagas starring James Stewart and directed by Anthony Mann (*Winchester '73* [1950], *Bend of the River* [1952], *The Naked Spur* [1953] and *The Man from Laramie* [1955]) and continued by Budd Boetticher with Randolph Scott in the lead role (*Seven Men from Now* [1956],

1. *Caine is Carter. Publicity photograph.*

Buchanan Rides Alone [1958], and *Ride Lonesome* [1959]). In *Get Carter*, too, the protagonist journeys to a wild place where 'a man has to do what a man has to do', in this case to avenge an attack on his family, even if it means his own death. In this 'north-eastern', the familiar iconography of the western genre is knowingly adapted to give New-castle a frontier quality: gangsters cruising the town in Jags stand in for gunslingers on horseback, drinks are knocked back in a long saloon bar, a shotgun rests on top of a wardrobe, there is a conspicuous presence of good-time girls and a conspicuous absence of lawmen. When a tough, taciturn loner rides into town, we know there is going to be business for the undertaker, just as we do in the 'spaghetti' westerns of Sergio Leone (*A Fistful of Dollars* [1964], *For a Few Dollars More* [1965], and *The Good, the Bad and the Ugly* [1966]).[6]

To think of the terraces and back alleys of Tyneside as merely substitutes for the mean streets of Los Angeles or Dodge City, however, is to ignore the fact that the generic roots of *Get Carter* run deep into European soil. Its theme of family revenge goes back to Greek classical drama and the tragedies of Seneca (*Thyestes*, *Medea* and *Agamemnon*), but its most salient ancestry is the dark and violent theatrical tradition of revenge tragedies that begins with Jacobean plays like John Webster's *The White Devil* (c. 1610) and *The Duchess of Malfi* (1612) and continues to be revived in films like *The Cook, the Thief, His Wife and Her Lover* (Peter Greenaway, 1988) and *Gangster No. 1* (Paul McGuigan, 2000). In Jacobean tragedy, the centre of violence and corruption is generally the court of the city state. *Get Carter* updates this trope by depicting Tyneside as a local state in which venality and the rule of force go largely unchallenged and, in Albany's words in *King Lear*, 'humanity must perforce prey upon itself'.[7]

The nihilistic mood of Jacobean tragedy, and its pessimistic depiction of an anomic society being eaten away from within, transfers easily to the dawn of the 1970s. Camus' description of the conditions in which tragedy thrives as a dramatic genre – an era in which 'man frees himself from an older form of civilization and finds that he has broken away from it without having found a new form which satisfies him' – is as relevant to the end of the 1960s as to the end of the sixteenth century.[8] Both were periods of transition in which dominant cultures and moralities were forced to give ground to emergent forces. *Get Carter*'s lawlessness recalls an earlier Elizabethan age in which medieval conceptions of personal honour and private justice were being challenged by the extension of state power and a public administration of justice.[9] Carter's is a 'blood revenge', the survival of a culturally sanctioned response to the murder of family members in the era before the codification of law and the universal authority of the state. And, like the Elizabethan dramatists before him, Hodges is careful to link the theme of revenge with an attack on the corruption endemic in the local state and the sense of a society disintegrating and out of control. As he once remarked, 'The film is not just about the villain. It's about observing the social structures and the deprivation of the country from which this character comes.'[10]

A similar vision of social dissolution and anomie had already been explored in Hollywood. Don Siegel had persuaded Clint Eastwood to discard his poncho to play a tough, unorthodox cop, a figure alienated from the city he visits in *Coogan's Bluff* (1968). Eastwood would play much the same role for Siegel in *Dirty Harry* (1971), a film made at roughly the same time as *Get Carter*. The closest affinities with Mike Hodges' film, however, are to be found in an American movie made by the British director John Boorman. In *Point Blank* (1967), a coldly violent thriller adapted from a Donald Westlake novel, Lee Marvin plays Walker, a professional criminal dedicated to avenging the wrongs done to him by his wife and her gangster lover. The film resembles *Get Carter* not only generally in its narrative structure, amoral atmosphere and sudden explosions of violence, but specifically in some of its textual details. Both films, for example, have a sequence in which a man is thrown from a tall building and either lands on, or narrowly misses, a car below, and both feature the shooting of a man named Carter by a sniper. In the case of *Point Blank*, Carter is a crime boss who proclaims that 'profit is the only principle', a doctrine to which Walker might also subscribe if he was not so obsessed with revenge.

Since the heyday of Al Capone in the late 1920s, American organised crime and its representation in Hollywood cinema have provided models of authenticity for British gangsters and crime film-makers alike. In spite of the fact that the literary and theatrical deep structures of the crime story are British and European in origin, the American colonisation of the generic terrain of the gangster film and its most authentic narrative and stylistic form – noir – have created a continuous challenge for British attempts to provide convincing representations of underworld activity. Consequently, the British crime film has been among the most assiduous promoters of an authentic impression of place and, by extension, a strong sense of national cultural identity in filmic representation. Given the association of crime with an urban underworld, the evocation of place has been primarily focused on the city. In the late 1940s, dramas like *It Always Rains on Sunday* (Robert Hamer, 1947), *Brighton Rock* (John Boulting, 1948), *The Blue Lamp* (Basil Dearden, 1949) and *Night and the City* (Jules Dassin, 1950) used location shooting to construct convincing portraits of the criminal milieu in London and the south of England. Ten years later, with the arrival of 'Angry Young Man' theatre and New Wave cinema, film-makers began to explore north of England settings. Val Guest took his cameras to Manchester for *Hell is a City* (1960) and Sidney Hayers went to Newcastle to shoot *Payroll* (1960).

Together with more illustrious counterparts such as *Room at the Top* (Jack Clayton, 1959) and *Saturday Night and Sunday Morning* (Karel Reisz, 1960), these films helped to direct attention to the northern conurbations as sites of both cinematic realism and social deprivation. In the emerging discourse of social progress, the cities of the north were cast as incubators of discontent, backward and puritanical enclaves that stifled the spirit and frustrated cultural and sexual desire. Ambition necessitated a move south to the more libertarian environs of London.

British cinema's realignment with the capital city is neatly summed up in the two John Schlesinger films *Billy Liar* (1963) and *Darling* (1965), which effectively follow the fortunes of the characters played by Julie Christie as she first breaks away from Bradford and then samples *la dolce vita* in London. British cinema's relationship to 'Swinging London', however, was a problematic one.[11] Left-liberal film-makers found it difficult to celebrate the wealth and hedonism London offered in the mid-1960s without unease and the residual feelings of guilt that are so often present in their movies. The long party that began when Julie Christie took the train to the capital in 1963 began to flag by the end of 1970. The Beatles had split, England had relinquished football's World Cup, and the Tories were back in power on a law-and-order ticket. One can sense a mood of desperation in *Smashing Time* (Desmond Davis, 1969), and the hangover is clearly evident in two British crime movies released in the same year as *Carter*: Donald Cammell and Nick Roeg's *Performance* (filmed in 1968) and Micheal Tuchner's *Villain*. Together with *Carter*, these films take stock of the criminal underworld in the wake of the Kray twins' imprisonment.

But *Get Carter* might equally belong to a short cycle of films that includes *Cool It Carol* (Pete Walker, 1970) and *The Reckoning* (Jack Gold, 1970), which take a jaundiced look at the relationships between metropolitan and provincial life. Although more overtly political than *Get Carter*, *The Reckoning* is strikingly similar in some of its iconography and narrative devices. An amoral northern boy, who has been successful in the city jungle of London, travels back to his home town and takes revenge for the death of a close relative, his father in this case. Like the Tyneside of *Get Carter*, the Merseyside of *The Reckoning* is presented as a wasteland of demolition sites and crumbling terraces. Stripped of a vital stimulus for progress by the migration of their brightest and best sons and daughters to the south, the once virile cities of the north have fallen into a slow decay. When the prodigal sons return, their drive to avenge the damage done to their families may be read as an attempt to assuage that guilt they suffer as deserters of the communities that nurtured them. Ted Lewis, the author of the book on which *Get Carter* was based, was one of these errant sons, leaving his Humberside home for a bright-lights job as an art director for a London advertising agency.

As a crime film, *Get Carter* occupies a place in what has been critically regarded as a subordinate tradition in British cinema, but it is also linked to dominant traditions by Wolfgang Suschitzky's naturalistic but imaginative cinematography. While the film's narrative approaches grand melodrama, much of its *mise-en-scène* is as realist as one might expect from a director and lighting cameraman with a background in documentaries. *Get Carter* demonstrates its classic documentary impulse in its desire for social exploration and its willingness to travel to a 'heart of darkness'. Like the nineteenth-century instigators of urban sociology and the early followers of pioneering documentary film-maker John Grierson's urge to 'tread dangerously into the jungles of Middlesbrough and the Clyde', Hodges and producer Michael Klinger led their cast and crew into the wastelands of Tyneside.[12] The poetic use of the realist style places *Get Carter* in a critically valorised strand of British cinema that runs from Robert Joseph Flaherty and Grierson through Reisz and Tony Richardson to Terence Davies. But, unlike much of the work in this tradition, *Carter* neither romanticises, celebrates nor encourages identification with the working-class community it so convincingly depicts. Here, the documentarist's gaze is neither pitying nor sentimental. Like J. B. Priestley's *English Journey* almost forty years previously, *Carter* takes a hard look at the north, softened only by wry humour and an underlying resentment of injustice. In his discussion of poetic realism, Andrew Higson argues that, above all, it must have 'emotional depth and integrity'[13] and, in *Get Carter*, Hodges overrides any impulse towards the heroic depiction of ordinary people in favour of the kind of 'imaginative truth' championed by Humphrey Jennings.[14] Forsaking the ideological certainties of 'moral realism', Hodges maintains the cool detachment of an anthropologist among cannibals. Rather than emphasising the warmth and good humour conventionally associated with northern urban life, he presents Newcastle as virtually a necropolis, a cheerless city of coffins and hearses where the locals are suspicious and hostile. Fear, intimidation and betrayal are their staple diet. Suschitzky uses the bleak industrial landscape of Tyneside to express an oppressive sense of dereliction and a poverty of the soul, contrasting the belching chimneys and grimy terraces with the tawdry glamour of the bingo and dance hall and the uncompromising concrete slabs that pass for redevelopment.

There is a match between the bleak and unsentimental moral universe that Carter inhabits and the world of civic corruption and neo-brutalism he visits, just as there is in American film noir. The film's vision of the New Britain is one in which municipal pride has been replaced by individual greed, beauty by barren ugliness. For Hodges, his film was sounding an alarm, warning the nation of how bad things were becoming:

> The country at that time had a totally hypocritical view of itself. It wasn't what it was pretending to be. We thought the police were wonderful, that corruption was only an American phenomenon and American gangsters were horrible and ours were nice. Once I'd decided to tell the truth, I had to do it with the same ruthlessness as a surgeon opening up a cancer patient, remove every article of sickness and reveal it for what it is.[15]

As in the bleakest of film noir, the world evoked by *Get Carter* is a predatory sea in which sharks prey on their own kind as well as the little fish. It is a cycle of death in which killers eventually become victims themselves. Michael Caine was himself conscious of how the class system under which he was brought up made it very difficult for the children of the terraces and tenements to break the cycle of replication: 'If you are born into that working-class milieu as I was and as virtually every violent criminal is, then you're sure to want something different. And if the world hits you violently enough, then you will act in a violent way to alter your circumstances.'[16]

Like film noir, too, *Get Carter* is fuelled by a dammed-up sexual energy that finds its release in violence and perversion. The first line of the film, 'bollock naked with his socks still on', sets the tone for its representation of sex as manipulative and consciously sordid. *Carter* turns the sexual libertarianism of its age on its head: 'free love' is not a way of escaping repression, but rather one of its instruments. Love in *Get Carter* is rarely free from the taint of self-interest or commercial exploitation. Sex is a means to power, not least for Carter, the son who obsessively challenges the authority of the father by bedding the lovers of all of the film's crime lords. The expelling of bodily fluids that takes place in Newcastle does not mean that the city should be viewed as a sexual playground but as a public convenience. The Jacobean tragedies that supplied the template for Carter's revenging exhibited what Salgado has described as an 'obsessive concentration on the purely animal aspects of human existence, eating, drinking, defecation and copulation',[17] and the

2. *The gangster and the gangster's moll. This publicity photograph of Michael Caine and Geraldine Moffat effectively connotes the film's genre.*

film shows a similar preoccupation with the basic functions of the body. Carter dismisses his home town as a 'craphouse', and toilets feature as much as bedrooms in the film. Con (George Sewell), the London hood sent to retrieve Carter, is locked in an outside privy, and Albert (Glynn Edwards), the reluctant porn star, is knifed outside one. Sewers, a common metaphor for the morally tainted criminal underworld, are never far from the surface in Hodges' vision of the city.

THE CHARACTER OF CARTER

'Injuries are not revenged except where they are exceeded.'[18] Seneca, *Thyestes*, II.195

Like Travis's crusade in *Taxi Driver* (Martin Scorsese, 1976), Carter's merciless assault on the rats of his urban sewer tackles the symptoms rather than the causes of moral decay and is inflected with the same hypocrisy. Carter apparently stands for the old world, the world of his childhood when family and community provided the city with a soul. His crusade is the reassertion, not of family values, but the value of family. The gangsters of Newcastle express their contempt for family relationships by murdering his brother and luring his niece/daughter into pornography. Carter sets out to make them regret this affront to his family name. But ironically, he, too, is infected with the malaise of his age. His value system is really little different from that of the men he pursues. He shows neither compassion for his victims nor much remorse for his crimes, and his hypocrisy about the value of the family is evidenced in his affair with his brother's wife. In truth, he is less family-centred than self-centred. The abuse of his family is a personal affront, a challenge to his own reputation as a hard man. Significantly, Hodges makes no attempt to show the event (the murder of Frank Carter) that triggers his protagonist's drive for vengeance. In this way, the director loosens the empathic bond that ties the viewer to the revenger in most dramas of this type. Carter's cold rage is never given the emotional support the depiction of the crime committed against his brother might draw from audiences. Moreover, Carter's fraternal relationship to the victim suggests that his wrath indexes loyalty due to another member of a homosocial order rather than the wider heterosocial order of the family.

Michael Caine saw his performance as an ethnographic exploration of the moral beliefs and social mores that underlie the gangster's presentation of self:

The problem with a lot of British gangster films is that the gangsters are portrayed either as funny or stupid. But real gangsters are neither. I should know, 'cos I grew up with them. The razor gangs down the Elephant and Castle. They're serious blokes. Serious and bright. And very scary. That's how I played Carter. Of course he's a villain. But he doesn't regard himself that way. He doesn't see himself as a bad man. He might do bad things. But he feels completely justified.[19]

Carter rails against the corrupt world but, ultimately, can transform neither the world nor himself. In this he strongly resembles the malcontent of Jacobean revenge tragedies, the figure Jonathan Dollimore labels the 'contradictory Jacobean anti-hero' and describes as:

> malcontented – often because bereaved or dispossessed – satirical and vengeful; at once agent and victim of social corruption, condemning yet simultaneously contaminated by it; made up of inconsistencies and contradictions which, because they cannot be understood in terms of individuality alone, constantly pressure attention outwards to the social contradictions of existence.[20]

Dollimore notes that the malcontent he is describing not only serves as a means of exposing a malaise at the heart of the social order, but constitutes 'a prototype of the modern discontented subject'.[21] Carter embodies Dollimore's contradictory revenger striding blindly out of the 1960s: a social sanitiser infected with the germs he seeks to sterilise, his righteousness compromised by his own corrupt morality. But this is no world for the righteous. Newcastle's mean streets are not for knights to go. Carter, unlike Raymond Chandler's Marlowe, is himself mean without the slightest trace of chivalry. He is more Mike Hammer than Philip Marlowe – frequently described by those he encounters (and sleeps with) as a 'bastard' – but Hodges likes to believe that the character retains the vestiges of a moral conscience: 'Carter had to be callous, but he knows he is sick, that he's not like normal people. When he sees the car [with a woman in the boot] tipped into the dock, I see regret in his face.'[22] The regret may not be obvious to all viewers, but the film's triumph is to raise this cold sociopath, against our better judgement, to the level of tragic hero. We might not go as far as Michael Caine did in a television interview and describe Carter as 'an upstanding citizen with the right moral values',[23] but we find it difficult not to side with this character who, after all, is the only candidate for sustained audience identification in the film. We find it hard not to respect Carter, although

3. *A family man? Caine with Petra Markham.*

he does nothing to deserve it. We are tempted to admire Carter, although there is nothing admirable in his behaviour. Our identification with the character is made guilty by the acknowledgement that we are colluding in murder. The revelation of *Get Carter* is the realisation of just how vulnerable our own moral codes have become. It was a revelation experienced by Hodges, himself, when he first viewed his creation with its intended audience: 'I had assumed that, like me, the audience would hate Carter and would also be shocked by the film. But what surprised and frightened me in many ways was that they actually liked him.'[24]

This identification with a protagonist in a way that entails the suspension of conventional morality is a typical mechanism of cult movie appreciation.[25] For the most part, Hodges scrupulously avoids standard mechanisms of identification like the point-of-view shot, and frequently adopts a mediated view of his protagonist, but identification is ultimately facilitated by the inevitability of the character's fate (subtly suggested by Hodges and evident after the initial viewing), and the feelings of social estrangement he embodies. Dollimore points to the importance of this sense of estrangement in his social-psychological profile of Vindice, the doomed protagonist of *The Revenger's Tragedy*.[26] Estrangement from society, Dollimore argues, provokes 'an aggressive reaction; heroic or criminal it adds up to the same thing: a desperate bid for integration'. This bid is futile, however, because characters like Vindice – or Carter – are bent on destroying 'that which they are within and which they cannot survive without'. The underworld is the air Carter breathes, and if he destroys or abandons it, he suffocates. This is why Dollimore argues that for the revenger to seek reintegration is to 'embrace destruction'. This is the 'vital irony' that supplies *Get Carter* with much of its fascination and underlies the 'subversive black camp' with which revengers' tragedies so often relieve their 'deep pessimism'.

It might be argued that the futility of Carter's crusade positions him as a classic film noir victim-hero. But if, in its moral bleakness and pessimism, the film resembles much of the noir canon, Carter's character breaks genre conventions. He is not the vulnerable man ensnared by a lethal spider woman, but a brick-hard killer who uses and abuses women as it suits him. Rather than a victim, he is a vortex that sucks all the characters he encounters into its downward spiral. His destruction conforms to the conventions of classical tragedy rather than to those of film noir. Carter is a victim of his 'fatal flaws', a manipulative and compassionless attitude to others, and an overbearing pride and arrogance that fuels his need to respond to any perceived affront and convinces him of his invulnerability. The faults in his character are a cipher for wider cultural ills, just as they are in Greek and Jacobean drama. As J. W. Lever wrote of the protagonists of tragedy in a book published in the same year *Get Carter* was released, 'the fundamental flaw is not in them but in the world they inhabit, in the political state, the social order it upholds'.[27] If Carter is redeemed it is not by his willingness to give love, or even by the sentimentality he shows towards his kith and kin, but by his status as martyr for the social order he represents.

Fatal though his flaws may be, they continue to exert a powerful attraction for audiences, not least because in other circumstances they could so easily be construed as virtues. Carter is brave and tenacious, unshakably committed to his chosen course of action and confident in its execution, but above all he exhibits 'a cool, flip, tough arrogance'[28] that links him to contemporary protagonists like Harry Callahan (*Dirty Harry*), Walker (*Point Blank*), and Coogan (*Coogan's Bluff*) and continues to recommend him to new generations of viewers. 'I modelled him on an actual hard case I once knew,' Caine once revealed. 'I watched everything the man did. I even saw him once put someone in hospital for eighteen months. Those guys are very polite, but they act right out of the blue. They're not conversationalists about violence, they're professionals.'[29]

THE CREATION OF CARTER

'You have to be ruthless. When you write you are drawing on your own emotions and relationships, your family and friends – and if this means you are exploiting people, well – it has to be done. My wife has come to terms with this now, I think – but my parents, for example, still find it painful to be "used".' Ted Lewis, interviewed in 1969.[30]

Jack Carter was the creation of Ted Lewis, a heavy-drinking commercial artist in his late twenties. Born in Manchester soon after the outbreak of World War II, he was brought up in Barton-on-Humber, where his father was a quarry manager. After attending Hull School of Art, he worked as a book illustrator, an animator and an art director at an advertising agency in London. In his spare time, he wrote stories with strongly autobiographical content. Hutchinson's publication of his first book, *All the Way Home and All the Night Through*, in 1965, encouraged his literary ambitions, and he began to devote an increasing proportion of his time to his second novel.[31]

Jack's Return Home was written in 1968, a year of political turmoil in which the established order was subjected to a sustained attack by a young intelligentsia. But, although Lewis's book may share some of the pent-up rage of the revolutionary left, it has none of its optimism or idealism. In spirit, it harks back two, three or even four decades to the hardboiled literary tradition of *Black Mask* magazine, and the radical cynicism of Dashiell Hammett and the sardonic detachment of Raymond Chandler. Lewis's prose has something of the simplicity and directness of Hammett and the world-weariness of Chandler, but his story also resembles the criminal-centred narratives of second-generation hardboiled writers like Jim Thompson and David Goodis. The book is written in the first person in the vernacular of Humberside, and manages to remain convincingly in character through to the end and the (probable) death of its narrator. In doing so, it conveys what Robert Murphy has called a 'provincial authenticity' that marries its American sensibilities to a line of British low-life thrillers by authors like James Curtis, Gerald Kersh and Arthur La Bern.[32]

The title *Jack's Return Home* suggests the completion of a circle – the cycle of birth and death, perhaps – but the book offers little reassurance in the rediscovery of the familiar. If it contrasts the unstable present with the securities of the past, it does so without much nostalgia. The past is a site of problems, the source of tensions in the present. Jack Carter's memories of growing up in and around the (unnamed) steel town of Scunthorpe are never sentimental, although they do recall a world before disillusionment, before his moral fall. Carter is cynical enough to describe his home town as 'a good place to say goodbye to', and clearly has contempt for most of its inhabitants, but, beneath this local antipathy and his general misanthropy, there is a nagging sense of loss and a need to set things right 'for the sake of past history'.[33] Some of this past history is apparent in the glimpses we are given of his relationship with his brother Frank in the austere 1940s, and the insights we gain into the reasons for their estrangement after Frank's marriage to a woman Carter had slept with on the eve of the wedding. The family trauma around the parenthood of Frank's daughter appears to have been at the root of Carter's decision to move to London, where he became a professional criminal, and the emotional autism that seems to have followed. Most of the emotions Jack expresses are about his child-hood. It is as if he has lost or repressed the ability to feel deeply about current acts and relationships, with the possible exception of his affair with his boss's wife, Audrey. When he learns that his boss has been informed of the affair, he tells us that his 'guts turned over', but the reason may be shock as much as any amorous bond.[34] Although he does not exhibit the 'authoritarian personality' of the classic fascist, the character with whom the first-person narration effectively encourages us to identify has a world-view that would not have been out of place in Nazi Germany: he believes that the ends justify the means, admires bullies, despises the weak, uses people for his own purposes, regards women with misogynistic suspicion and yet valorises the idea of the family. Certainly, it is made clear that he kills without compassion or remorse as the following passage illustrates: 'I looked down at Peter and stretched my arm out and pointed the shooter at his head. He stared up at me. His mind was almost gone with pain, but not enough not to know he was going to die. I shot him through the forehead and walked over to the TR4.'[35]

The starkness of the prose is matched by the bleakness of the moral and behavioural world it describes. It is a parallel world of duplicity, conspiracy, egotism and sudden death that sucks in and entraps its participants, and it festers beneath the surface of even a small provincial town. In this world, the centres of power are difficult to locate, and the course of justice is rerouted by secret and venal relationships. Formal and legitimate authority is responsive to neither the needs of the people, nor the rule of law, but to the contradictory pressures of systemic corruption and fear of exposure. Consequently, justice is done only when it is in the spotlight and must be seen to be done. The Humberside of *Jack's Return Home* – and, by implication, much of the rest of the country – harbours an undiagnosed sickness. The local state is secretly subject to the influence of 'the governors', a shadowy network of crime bosses, with links to London gangland, which also controls many apparently legitimate businesses. Although Lewis never names Scunthorpe, its identity is encoded in the names given to some of his characters: the cowardly (Scun)Thorpe and the ambitious Brumby (the name of the central business district of Scunthorpe).

In writing his novel, Lewis was working through the unresolved conflicts of his own early years. In Carter, he created a fantasy alter ego to express the ruthlessness he admired in a writer but struggled to find in himself.[36] His widow has recalled that he had little discipline when it came to his work routines, and remained needful of the approval of his father.[37] Although Lewis's novel is a serious work, it was written as an 'entertainment', to use Graham Greene's term, and conceived primarily as a commercial venture rather than a piece of social criticism. Lewis wanted to be a popular rather than a literary author, but he also craved critical recognition, as his distressed response to a negative reader's report at Michael Joseph testifies.[38] There were few British antecedents, however, to prepare critics or readers for the unsettling journey to the dark side of Humberside provided by *Jack's Return Home*. It is an uncompromising book that supplies the reader with few clues for its interpretation. With the exception of Keith the barman, there are hardly any characters who demonstrate attractive qualities and, while most may not quite deserve their fate, few earn our sympathy. Whereas Graham Greene, a novelist admired by Lewis, had used the gangster narrative to explore moral philosophy in books such as *Brighton Rock* (1938), Lewis withholds judgement on the underworld he so vividly evokes. His book generates the sort of moral vacuum that George Orwell condemned James Hadley Chase for creating in his notorious *No Orchids for Miss Blandish* (1939).[39] *No Orchids*, however, was set in the USA, and much of the shock of Lewis's novel comes from its location in a familiar and believable English town – not the already infamous flesh pots of Brighton, but the sort of ordinary, working-class place written about by the northern realist school. The achievement of *Jack's Return Home* at the end of the 1960s was to make its readers look at a town like Scunthorpe anew, to see below the surface. It is tempting to argue that it encouraged readers to question the myth of working-class respectability propagated by Richard Hoggart's *Uses of Literacy*,[40] but its attitude to working-class consumerism and the social changes wrought by postwar affluence is too ambivalent for that. Its middle-aged villains, however, are vivid enough to suggest that, at a time of significant youthful dissent, young people were not the only threat to social order.

The man who would bring *Jack's Return Home* to the screen, independent producer Michael Klinger, was a unique figure in the British film industry. He was a showman able to bridge the sizeable gap between commercial sexploitation and a cinema of genuine artistic experimentation. The son of a Polish tailor, Klinger was born in Soho in 1920 and thoroughly imbibed its ethos of rule-breaking and shrewd deal-making. He started out as a disc jockey, but by the late 1950s, he was cashing in on the Soho striptease boom by managing the Nell Gwynne club. The club's performers supplied much of the subject matter for the epidemic of 8mm 'glamour' films that began to be produced for the home-viewing market at the time, and would later feature in the plot of *Get Carter*. It was at the Nell Gwynne that Klinger met Tony Tenser, then head of publicity for Miracle Films, a UK distributor for racy continental pictures. In 1960 they went into partnership and opened the Compton Cinema Club to show uncertificated movies to a 'sophisticated' membership. As Compton-Cameo Films, they quickly branched out into film distribution and production, beginning with naturist epics like Harrison Marks' *Naked as Nature Intended* (1961), and taking the fading British social problem cycle in a more consciously exploitative direction with cautionary tales such as *That Kind of Girl* (Robert Hartford-Davis, 1963) and *The Yellow Teddybears* (Hartford-Davis, 1963). The following year, Compton-Cameo extended its portfolio by backing the mondo documentaries being made by Stanley Long and Arnold Louis Miller: *London in the Raw* (1964), *Primitive London* (1965) and the docu-drama *Secrets of a Windmill Girl* (1965).

Its ability to supply a niche market with titillating fare was fast making Compton-Cameo one of the most financially successful independent companies in British film-making, but Klinger was to demonstrate that his interest in cinema went deeper than catch-penny sensationalism by backing the talent of a promising director from his father's homeland. The production of Roman Polanski's *Repulsion* (1965) and *Cul-de-sac* (1966), followed by Peter Collinson's obtuse and Pinteresque *The*

Penthouse (1968), established Klinger as a cineaste and risk-taker to complement his reputation as a showman and deal-maker. *The Penthouse* was Klinger's first solo production after his split with Tenser, and was quickly followed by *Baby Love* (Alastair Reid, 1968), the controversial story of a suburban Lolita. In 1969, with the conviction of the Kray brothers making headlines, Klinger decided that it was time to produce a tough gangster picture. His friend the producer/director Peter Walker had been quicker off the mark with his own low-budget crime film *Man of Violence* (1970), filmed in the summer of 1969. Klinger was invited to view the first print of the film with Walker later in the year and, after informing its director that it was 'a load of old crap, son', he announced, 'I'm going to make a gangster film, but it's going to cost a lot more than this and it's going to be better.'[41] A trawl of publishers for suitable properties turned up *Jack's Return Home*, and Klinger recognised its potential immediately. His creative imagination quickly linked the book to the promise shown by a new writer-director whose work Klinger had seen on Thames Television a few nights earlier, on 17 November 1969. The programme was an eighty-minute filmed teleplay entitled *Suspect*, and its creator was Mike Hodges. The jigsaw that was to be *Get Carter* was beginning to fall into place.

As the project germinated in Klinger's mind, his friend Robert Littman was made head of European production at MGM. The Hollywood giant had been a significant force in British production for decades, but, with the single exception of *Blow-up* (Michelangelo Antonioni, 1967), it had failed to cash in on the bonanza of 'Swinging London', maintaining a conservative policy of financing apparently safe projects by established (and usually ageing) directors. The success of Kubrick's *2001: A Space Odyssey* (1968) kept the operation afloat for a while, but with the failures of *Goodbye Mr Chips* (Herbert Ross, 1969) and *Alfred the Great* (Clive Donner, 1969) it was shipping water at an alarming rate.[42] Littman's appointment represented a last desperate attempt to bail out the Euro-liner with cheap but commercial projects. Littman asked Klinger if he had any properties in development that might be suitable for the Hollywood fleet's sinking ship, and was quickly sold the idea of *Get Carter*. With a projected budget of less than £1 million it looked a solid investment. The agreement was hatched in the nick of time. In February 1970, MGM's new managing director announced the closure of the company's Boreham Wood Studios and its British operations. If the announcement had come two months earlier, *Get Carter* might never have been made. In any case, the imminent collapse of MGM's interest in British production lent the making of *Get Carter* a sense of urgency that would bring the project to completion in record time: nine months. With Littman's backing, and following a discussion with Mike Hodges' agent Barry Krost, Klinger mailed the proofs of *Jack's Return Home* to his chosen director with a note inviting him to consider turning the book into a film that he might like to handle.[43]

Mike Hodges came from a very different background from both Michael Klinger and Ted Lewis. He was brought up in comfortable circumstances in the west of England, qualifying as a chartered account-ant at the age of twenty-two in 1955. But after his National Service, he decided to turn his back on accountancy and try his luck in the television industry as a teleprompter operator. By the early 1960s, Hodges had written his first television play and, ironically for an atheist socialist, had been appointed as the editor of an ABC Television religious programme for young people. After an abortive attempt to make a documentary on Stephen Ward and the Profumo affair, Hodges successfully pitched an idea for a film on undertakers to Granada's *World in Action*, and began a two-year association with the programme. Between 1963 and 1965, he travelled widely, making programmes in Canada, the USA and Vietnam, before transferring to the ITV arts programme *Tempo*, where he made profiles of designers, writers and film directors including Orson Welles and Jean-Luc Godard. The profiles were made in the style of their subject, and Hodges further experimented with form in his contributions to a series of films on media culture. By the time Ted Lewis was working on *Jack's Return Home*, however, Hodges was also ready to work on a thriller because, as he told Mark Adams, 'Done well they can be like an autopsy of society. Crime is a wonderful way of really looking at what is going on.'[44] The result was *Suspect*, the film that brought him to Klinger's attention.

Mike Hodges received the proofs of Lewis's novel on 28 January 1970 and knew very soon after starting to read that this was a project that he wanted to take on.[45] As Hodges set to work on his script, Klinger's mind turned to the question of a star for the film. With the confidence afforded by the involvement of a Hollywood major, he approached Michael Caine's agent Dennis Selinger. His timing was impeccable. Hodges' second Thames Television play *Rumour* had been broadcast (2 March 1970) while the proposal was being considered and had been greeted with enthusiasm by both Caine and Selinger. As Hodges has recalled, this second film for the *Playhouse* series was more experimental than *Suspect* had been: 'I used flash-forwards (shot in the Blackwell tunnel in London) as an image of a descent into Hell, slow motion, jump cuts, it was very much *nouvelle vague* style.'[46] The film, with its sardonic voiceover, captured the cynicism of the new decade, the profound loss of faith in established institutions like the press, and the gathering climate of sleaze, corruption and sadism. By early March, Caine was on board and Hodges, already beginning to earn his modest fee of £7,000 as writer and director, had delivered the first draft of his script.

Having never attempted to adapt any text before, Hodges was inclined to stick as closely as possible to Lewis's novel, but soon realised that he had to prioritise its cinematic possibilities. Dropping Lewis's title and substituting *Carter's the Name*, his treatment retained the essential structure of Lewis's novel with its strong narrative drive, but introduced some minor changes to characterisation and more fundamental alterations to narratology. Most significantly, Hodges decided to avoid the then unfashionable conventions of film noir by dispensing with the voiceover suggested by the book's first-person narration, and to use any flashbacks indicated by Carter's memories of his early years as almost subliminal flash edits. In this way, he streamlined and modernised the story-telling style, confining the action to the long weekend Carter spends in his home town, and adopting a more detached and observational mode of reportage to replace the book's impressionism. The immediate consequence was the loss of the insights into Carter's motivations provided by his memories of boyhood and his relationships with brother Frank and delinquent gang leader Albert Swift. Also lost was the backstory of Carter's dealings with Eric Paice during their time as rival gangsters in London, in particular, Eric's violent treatment of Carter's lover Audrey (renamed Anna in the screenplay), the memory of which fuels Carter's hatred. In place of exposition and the development of subsidiary characters, Hodges would decide, during filming, to emphasise the cyclical and inevitable nature of the story by scattering it liberally with *mementi mori*, including the trope of placing the man who turns out to be Carter's nemesis in the same carriage on the journey north.[47] In fact, Hodges had to fight hard for his preferred ending against his financiers at MGM, who would have liked the protagonist to survive for a possible sequel.

Hodges saw his film as a tragedy in the tradition of Elizabethan drama and grand opera, rather than as an action thriller. It would, however, be a tragedy anchored to real contemporary social conditions, and would tap into the rage of the times. The screenplay was written in a climate of disintegrating social order. Persistent rioting in Ulster had brought British Army intervention and the formation of the Provisional

IRA, and in England there was widespread student unrest, including bombings and violent demonstrations. The press was gripped by a moral panic about the activities of 'skinheads', and 'queer-bashing' and 'Paki-bashing' entered the language. As 1970 began, Britain was experiencing a spate of bank robberies, and its first case of abduction for gain. In the aftermath of the Kray twins' imprisonment, it was an active time for gangland, with the killing of Eddie Coleman in March. It was this apparently accelerating descent into disorder that helped sweep the Conservative Party to power in the summer's general election, and informed a number of contemporary film-makers' explorations of the morality of violence. While Hodges planned *Get Carter*, Kubrick was making *A Clockwork Orange* (1972), Ken Russell was working on *The Devils* (1971), and Sam Peckinpah was developing *Straw Dogs* (1971).[48]

Hodges' most fundamental transformation of Lewis's novel had nothing to do with narrative and characterisation. It was, of course, the relocation of the action from Humberside to Tyneside. In the spring of 1970 Klinger, Hodges and driver Reg Niven set off in the producer's Cadillac to scout east coast locations, to find a suitable place to represent Jack's home town, 'the blast furnace where his hardness and anger was cast'.[49] As a television auteur, Hodges had previously researched his locations alone and unobtrusively in his old Fiat. The process had allowed him time to think and to develop ideas for his production. This time, he was in an ostentatious American gas-guzzler with a producer who had his own ideas about settings and treatments. Although Lewis's novel is set in an inland steel town, Hodges was looking for somewhere more familiar to him, and somewhere with the added cinematic appeal of the sea. He already had indelible memories of the fishing ports he had visited during his national service in the Royal Navy's Fishery Protection Fleet, but he discovered that, thirteen years on, most of them had been 'decimated by developers'.[50] He had high hopes of Hull, but like Jack returning home, he found that things had changed. In the aftermath of the post-war economic boom, much of the crumbling seediness nurtured by austerity had been swept away, replaced by glass and concrete developments. Discouraged, Hodges was about to call off the search and settle for the tried and tested Nottingham (*Saturday Night and Sunday Morning*, Karel Reisz, 1960) when he remembered docking on Tyneside in the mid-1950s and decided to see if its character had escaped the planners:

> We pressed on and came to Newcastle. The visual drama of the place

took my breath away. Seeing the great bridges crossing the Tyne, the waterfront, the terraced houses stepped up each side of the deep valley, I knew that Jack was home. And although the developers were breathing down the Scotswood Road, they hadn't yet gobbled it up. We'd got there in time. But only just.[51]

Satisfied that they had found the right setting for the film, Michael Klinger headed back to London in his Caddy, leaving his director to complete the fine details of location spotting. Fired with fresh enthusiasm and given a free hand by his producer, Hodges set to work modifying his script to exploit the visual possibilities offered by Tyneside. Whereas Lewis's setting had been a small town and the surrounding sprawl of impoverished countryside and pretentious suburbs, the film's would be the claustrophobic canyon of Newcastle, a city with one foot in the past and one in the future. Lewis's nondescript pubs and farmsteads would be replaced as scenes of action by the more cinematic locations around the Tyne.[52]

With a script in place and principal locations sourced, Hodges and Klinger assembled a highly talented creative team. Hodges had been impressed by Ken Hughes' *The Small World of Sammy Lee* (1963) and knew that he wanted the cinematographer responsible for giving the film its poetic documentary aesthetic: Wolfgang Suschitzky. The veteran Viennese cameraman had worked in continental Europe as a photographer before World War II, finally coming to England in 1937. He had immediately struck up a partnership with Paul Rotha to make documentaries. Their work during the war included *World of Plenty* (1943) and government-sponsored magazine programmes and information shorts. His introduction into feature film-making had been in Rotha's critically acclaimed *No Resting Place* (1951), one of the first British features shot entirely on location. He had gone on to photograph another Colin Lesslie production, *The Oracle* (USA: *The Horse's Mouth*, Pennington Richards, 1952), another Rotha film, *Cat and Mouse* (1958), and Jack Clayton's Oscar-winning short film, *The Bespoke Overcoat* (1955), developing a reputation as an expert location photographer with a documentarist's ability to extract atmosphere from naturalistic settings. In the 1960s his commissions had ranged from Joseph Strick's controversial *Ulysses* (1967) to Hammer's *Vengeance of She* (Cliff Owen, 1968). His last film before *Carter* was *Entertaining Mr. Sloane* (Douglas Hickox, 1970). Suschitzky's camera operator would be Dusty Miller, who would go on to be Euston Films' leading cinematographer, endlessly photographing the landscape of Greater London for the TV series *The Sweeney*, *Minder* and *The Professionals*.

Suschitzky and Miller's footage would be assembled by the safe hands of John Trumper, an editor well versed in the rhythms of cutting thrillers, which constituted the majority of the thirty features he had edited in the previous twenty years. Trumper's recent experience covered work with directors with such divergent styles as Peter Watkins (*Privilege*, 1967) and Peter Collinson (*The Italian Job*, 1969). He had just cut Suschitzky's footage for *Entertaining Mr. Sloane*. *Get Carter*'s production design would be handled by Assheton Gorton, who had begun his career in television but was most closely associated with high 1960s films such as *The Knack* (Richard Lester, 1965), *Blow-up*, *The Magic Christian* (Joseph McGrath, 1969), and *Wonderwall* (Joe Massot, 1968). *Carter* would offer few of the opportunities for flamboyant creativity Gorton had enjoyed on productions like these.

CASTING *CARTER*

'... we observe in tragedies
That a good actor many times is curs'd
For playing a villain's part ...'

Ferdinand in John Webster, *The Duchess of Malfi*,
IV.ii.282–4

Michael Caine (Jack Carter)   When Hodges was working on the first draft of his script, he had Ian Hendry in mind for the role of Carter, only to discover that Michael Caine had been recruited for the part while the ink was still wet on the script. 'Jack Carter was such a shit it never occurred to me that a star would risk his reputation playing him.'[53] After a slow start to his screen acting career, Caine's star was very much in the ascendant. He had become *the* male face of British cinema in the 1960s, an icon popularised by David Bailey and a string of leading roles in successful movies. Caine had his own interpretation of Carter's character, and would significantly modify Hodges' formulation of his protagonist as a seedy but tough wide boy. Caine would give him a cold authority that is implicit in Lewis's original conception. As Hodges recalled:

> In the script, Carter was softer and sleazier than he was in the final film. But Michael Caine gave him an edge – he really knew Carter and made him more ruthless. Remember when he's in that Newcastle bar and he

asks for his drink – 'in a thin glass'? [...] In the script Carter says 'Please'. But Michael left it out and that little choice just makes Carter even more terrifying.[54]

For Caine, playing Carter was also something of a return home. Shortly before taking the part, he had made a nostalgic trip back to the area of south London in which he had grown up, discovering, in the process, that the Kennington Regal cinema in which he had spent so many contented hours truanting from school was being demolished. It was a time of taking stock of his roots and the trajectory of his career.[55] The role of Carter was not only business, it was personal. Carter represented the path sinister he had managed to avoid taking in his adolescence. As he remarked, 'Carter is the dead-end product of my own environment, my childhood. I know him well. He is the ghost of Michael Caine.'[56] Caine's identification with the character would be signified by the rejection of any attempt to simulate a Geordie accent. This was entirely in keeping with Hodges' dialogue, which paid no attention to specifically north-eastern speech patterns. Caine's natural London accent was perfectly acceptable to his director: 'I thought it fair to assume that Carter had been in London long enough to master the accent.'[57]

The force of Caine's performance, however, would derive, in part, from the way in which it contradicted or extended his established star persona. In contrast to the assertion of the film's publicity that 'Caine is Carter', the actor's roles had evoked a rather more humorous and vulnerable character than the cold killer he played in this film. His most celebrated role had probably been as the eponymous *Alfie* (1964), the working-class playboy in Lewis Gilbert's tragi-comedy of manners, and his image as an artful dodger had been enhanced by his recent leading part in *The Italian Job*. Jack Carter was a very different kettle of fish. Caine once described Harry Palmer, the character he played in *The Ipcress File* (Sidney J. Fury, 1965) as 'a winner who comes on like a loser'.[58] Carter is a loser who comes on like a winner. Making *Carter* would prove a sufficiently winning experience for Caine to form a production partnership with Hodges and Klinger – 'The Three Michaels' – to make a second film, *Pulp* (Mike Hodges, 1972). Almost unbelievably, Caine's stand-in on *Get Carter* would be a man named Jack Carter.

Ian Hendry (Eric Paice)   Thirty-nine-year-old Ian Hendry had been obliged to take up auctioneering and estate management in his native

4. *A forceful performance. Caine practises his phone manner.*

Suffolk before finally persuading his father to allow him to become an actor. After a spell in rep, he had secured parts in *Simon and Laura* (Muriel Box, 1955), *The Secret Place* (Clive Donner, 1956) and *Room at the Top* (Jack Clayton, 1959), before landing leading roles in television in *Police Surgeon* (1960) and in the first series of the legendary *The Avengers* (1961). By 1962, Hendry had become a 'hot property' in British film-making and starred in *Live Now, Pay Later* (Jay Lewis, 1962), *This is My Street* (Sidney Hayers, 1963), *Girl in the Headlines* (USA: *The Model Murder Case*, Michael Truman, 1963) and *The Beauty Jungle* (USA: *Contest Girl*, Val Guest, 1964). The films were not the box-office hits they had been expected to be, however, and by 1965, as Michael Caine's star rose, Hendry began to slip back to supporting actor status in films like *The Hill* (Sidney Lumet, 1965), *The Sandwich Man* (Robert

Hartford-Davis, 1966) and *The McKenzie Break* (Lamont Johnson, 1970). He had first worked for Michael Klinger when he played the sexist Michael in Polanski's *Repulsion*. By the time he took the part of Kinnear's odious lieutenant, Eric, in *Get Carter*, Hendry's problems with alcohol were obvious, his image was becoming more seedy, and his career was sliding faster downhill. In the 1970s he would be largely confined to character parts in exploitation movies like *Intimate Games* (Tudor Gates, 1976) and *The Bitch* (Gerry O'Hara, 1979). Just before his death in 1984, he would accept a small role in the Channel 4 television soap *Brookside*.

Britt Ekland (Anna Fletcher)   Swedish actress Britt Ekland was already a familiar face, both on screen and in the gossip columns, when she was offered the role of Anna, gang boss Gerald Fletcher's adulterous wife. After leading roles in continental films, she had come to England to work in television, and went on to appear in a string of feature films that developed her reputation as a sex symbol. A marriage to Peter Sellers was soon followed by a divorce in 1968, but her career continued to prosper. She won roles in American movies such as *The Night They Raided Minsky's* (William Friedkin, 1968) and *Stiletto* (Bernard Kowalski, 1969). When it came to casting *Get Carter*, her familiarity to US audiences recommended her to MGM, while her pairing with Michael Caine promised some interesting sexual chemistry. Consequently, she was given a prominence in the film's publicity that was hardly warranted by the size of her role. Having already played two gangsters' molls, however, Ekland was concerned about becoming typecast.[59]

John Osborne (Cyril Kinnear)   In a radical piece of casting, Hodges persuaded the famous playwright John Osborne to play the Godfather of Tyneside, Cyril Kinnear. Osborne had begun his career as an actor in the early 1950s before writing the celebrated play *Look Back in Anger* (1956) and launching the 'angry young man' cycle of novels and plays. As a founding partner of Woodfall Films, he had adapted his own plays for the British screen, and produced the acclaimed adapted screenplay for *Tom Jones* (Tony Richardson, 1963), but *Get Carter* was his first acting role in a British film. For Osborne, his role represented an opportunity to take a break from writing and to recharge his batteries. His part as a sophisticated, middle-aged crime lord would also help to shake off his lingering image as an *enfant terrible*. 'I hope people have forgotten that "angry young man" image which became rather tiresome in the end.'[60] His casting meant a distinct change to Lewis's original conception of Kinnear as a squat, obese and uncultured spiv. Not only was Osborne tall, slim and bearded, he also saw his character as a fallen member of legitimate society rather than a risen member of the criminal classes:

> He's a villain, and villains are always fun to play. He's a big-time provincial crook. A big fish in a small pond. Kinnear has pretensions too. He's the type of man who's been a Warrant Officer in the Army and then wears a Brigade of Guards Regimental tie in later years. But he has a sense of humour which makes him human.[61]

On location, Osborne was something of a private figure, but Hodges has commented that he really enjoyed his part: 'he had that sort of calmness about him of the truly powerful'.[62] The most challenging aspect of the role, however, turned out to be the need to give a convincing performance as a poker player. Unfamiliar with most card games, Osborne spent hours practising poker before his gambling scene.[63] Hodges would later coax Osborne back before the cameras for his *Flash Gordon* (1980).

Tony Beckley (Peter the Dutchman)   Since making his feature film debut at the age of thirty-eight in Orson Welles' *Chimes at Midnight* (1965), Southampton-born Tony Beckley had been consistently in demand with casting directors, making something of a specialism playing criminal types. He had been disturbingly convincing as one of the sadists who terrorise a young couple in Michael Klinger's production *The Penthouse*, and would shortly go on to star as the religious psychopath in *The Fiend* (Robert Hartford-Davis, 1971). His most enduring portrayal, however, would prove to be Camp Freddie in Peter Collinson's *The Italian Job*, the film on which he had first worked with Michael Caine. In *Get Carter* he was given another 'camp' role as Peter, the unstable London hood who is more clearly characterised in Lewis's novel as a misogynistic homosexual.

George Sewell (Con McCarty)   As the man who had introduced Barbara Windsor to Charles Kray, George Sewell was a natural choice to play a London gangster. In his mid-forties in 1970, Sewell had come to acting late. Son of a London print worker, he had begun to follow in his father's footsteps before joining the RAF and then the Merchant Navy. By the time he jokingly tried his hand at acting in Joan Littlewood's Theatre Workshop in 1959, he had worked in jobs as varied as travel courier, bricklayer, barman, street photographer, dance-band drummer and manager of a roller-skating team. His first film role was in Littlewood's *Sparrows Can't Sing* (1963), a film in which the Kray brothers took a paternal interest. By the time he was cast in *Get Carter*, he was a veteran of crime dramas like *Robbery* (Peter Yates, 1967) and BBC's *Z Cars*, and of social realist film-making by Lindsay Anderson and Ken Loach, having acted in *This Sporting Life* (Anderson, 1963), *Cathy Come Home* (Loach, BBC 1965) and *Poor Cow* (Loach, 1967). Together with Dorothy White, Sewell had already worked with Hodges on the television play *Suspect*. He had recently appeared regularly on television in the space opera *UFO*, and would shortly take a leading part in the *Special Branch* series. He continues to be a familiar face on TV in the twenty-first century.

Geraldine Moffat (Glenda) Geraldine Moffat's stunning looks and ability to personify the 1960s 'dolly bird' have unfortunately caused observers to overlook the quality of her acting. In fact, the Nottingham-born actress was far from being some ingenue recruited to play a good-time girl solely because of the shapeliness of her legs in a mini-skirt. She had trained at the prestigious Old Vic Theatre School in Bristol, and had a wealth of experience in repertory and on the West End stage. She had made her film debut in *The Man Who Had Power Over Women* (John Krish, 1970), but it was her work in television drama, particularly her leading roles in the Alun Owen teleplays *Stella* and *Doreen*, that caught the attention of Mike Hodges. Before retiring from acting to bring up her rock musician sons, Moffat would continue to make guest appearances in TV action series like *Jason King* and *The Persuaders*, ending her career as a barmaid in *Coronation Street* (1980).

Dorothy White (Margaret) Apart from an uncredited appearance in a 1955 film *Touch and Go* (Michael Truman), the role of the adulterous Margaret, Frank Carter's lover, was Dorothy White's first on the big screen. After studying drama in her spare time and joining Birmingham Rep, she had gone on to forge a successful career as a television actress, notably in BBC's *Z Cars*. White had first worked with Hodges on his teleplay *Suspect*. After *Get Carter*, she made one more film appearance (*Family Life*, Ken Loach, 1972), before returning to television.

Rosemarie Dunham (Edna Garfoot) Rosemarie Dunham made her (credited) film debut as Carter's randy landlady. Born in Scotland to a

Greek mother and English father, she spent much of her early life in Malta before beginning her acting career in English repertory. In the early 1960s, she spent two years in the Old Vic Company, and one of her first television roles was in an episode of *The Avengers* (1964). After *Get Carter*, she worked regularly in television, including a part in *Coronation Street*, until the early 1980s. Mike Hodges would bring her back to the big screen in 1998 in *Croupier*.

Petra Markham (Doreen) Although she had little previous feature film experience, Petra Markham was a mature twenty-four-year-old when she took on the role of Carter's sixteen-year-old niece. Sister of fellow actress Kika Markham, she had appeared in productions at the Royal Court and the Roundhouse, and in television shows as varied as *The Marty Feldman Show* and *The Wednesday Play*. With only four scenes in *Get Carter*, she was able to juggle the requirements of location filming with her theatre work at the Royal Court and her role in the television series *Victoria and Albert*. She continued to work mainly on the small screen after *Get Carter*, and is best known for her role as Rose Chapman, the wife murdered by her gangster husband in BBC's *EastEnders*. In 1999 she was reunited with Rosemarie Dunham in *Out of Depth* (Simon Marshall, 2001), a thriller photographed by Wolfgang Suschitzky's grandson Adam.

Bryan Mosley (Cliff Brumby) Although MGM originally had Telly Savalas in mind for the part of the slot machine magnate Cliff Brumby, *Coronation Street* actor Bryan Mosley was cast after executives were impressed by his acting in fight scenes from *Far from the Madding Crowd* (John Schlesinger, 1968).[64] Mosley was an accomplished performer in stage fights, and proved ideal casting for the big man in bad shape. When offered the part, however, he reacted with a mixture of excitement and apprehension. Afraid that participating in such a violent film might compromise his Catholic faith, Mosley took the script to his local priest and waited anxiously for his verdict:

> A few days later the priest returned with his conclusion. I was pretty astounded when he said he thought it was a very good morality play! The tone of the piece, although violent, did not condone such actions – indeed, even condemned them. I was relieved and at peace with the decision to go ahead.[65]

As well as appearing as Alf Roberts in more than 3,000 episodes of *Coronation Street*, and acting in hundreds of television dramas and stage plays, Mosley had parts in a number of feature films before making a decision to concentrate on work for the small screen. A native of Leeds, his cinema career began in the New Wave films set in Yorkshire: *A Kind of Loving* (John Schlesinger, 1962) and *This Sporting Life*. Other film appearances included *The Rattle of a Simple Man* (Betty Box, 1974), *Up Jumped a Swagman* (Christopher Miles, 1965), *Privilege*, and *30 is a Dangerous Age, Cynthia* (Joe McGrath, 1967).

Glynn Edwards (Albert Swift) Like George Sewell, Glynn Edwards entered the acting profession in his thirties through Joan Littlewood's Theatre Workshop, and made one of his first screen appearances in *Sparrows Can't Sing*. He had subsequently become a familiar face (most often as a policeman) in British films and television, having already acted alongside Michael Caine in *Zulu* and *The Ipcress File*. After playing Albert the part-time porn star in *Get Carter*, Edwards would be regularly employed as a character actor, most memorably playing Dave, the manager of the Winchester Club in the *Minder* television series.

Bernard Hepton (Thorpe) Bradford-born Bernard Hepton had established a successful career as both an actor and television producer when Hodges persuaded him to take the part of Kinnear's nervous messenger in *Get Carter*. One of Hepton's most recent television roles had been as Caiaphas, High Priest of Jerusalem, in Dennis Potter's controversial *Son of Man* (1969). In fact, he made something of a specialisation in playing priests, taking the role of Archbishop Cranmer in the blockbuster television series *The Six Wives of Henry VIII* and *Elizabeth R*, both screened in the year of *Get Carter*'s release, 1971. He reprised the role in the film version of *The Six Wives*, two years later, and went on to appear in *Barry Lyndon* (Stanley Kubrick, 1975) and *Gandhi* (Richard Attenborough, 1982), but he probably remains best known for two other roles in hit TV series: Toby Esterhase in the adaptations of John Le Carré's *Tinker, Tailor, Soldier, Spy* (1980) and *Smiley's People* (1982), and Albert Foiret in *Secret Army* (1977) and *Kessler* (1981).

Alun Armstrong (Keith) Alun Armstrong would eventually play his most famous role twenty-five years after *Get Carter* in another Newcastle-set drama, *Our Friends in the North* (1996). In that celebrated television series, he would revisit the roots of corruption in the north east of the 1960s as the local Labour politician, Austin Donohue. When Hodges cast him as Carter's victimised helper, he was making his screen debut.

Terence Rigby (Gerald Fletcher) Like so many of the actors selected by Hodges to give *Get Carter* an authentic feel, thirty-three-year-old Terence Rigby was best known for his work in television drama, having appeared in crime series such as *Softly Softly*, *The Saint* and *Callan*. His single film credit was as a policeman in Joseph Losey's *Accident* (1967). Since appearing briefly as the crime lord Gerald Fletcher, Rigby has enjoyed a distinguished career as a character actor on stage and screen, featuring in *Our Friends in the North*, and British films such as *Elizabeth* (Kapur, 1998), *Plunkett and Macleane* (Jake Scott, 1999) and *Essex Boys* (Terry Winsor, 2000).

John Bindon (Sid Fletcher) The son of a London taxi driver, John 'Biffo' Bindon was 'discovered' by Ken Loach in a west London pub and recruited as an untried supporting actor to Carole White and Terence Stamp in *Poor Cow*. He went on to establish a career in films and television playing crooks and cheeky chappies, notably in *Quadrophenia* (Franc Roddam, 1979). Although still in his twenties in 1970, Bindon's credentials to play the small role of the gang boss Sid Fletcher were impeccable. He had an intimate knowledge of the underworld, having spent part of his youth in Borstal and most of his adult life associating with criminals. By the end of the 1960s, he had charmed his way into the inner circles of swinging London, hobnobbing with top models and royalty. His career would take a nose-dive in the mid-1970s when he became involved in protection racketeering in Fulham and was acquitted of murder at the Old Bailey. A string of convictions for violence would follow before his death in penury in 1993.[66]

Other Parts For the film's minor supporting roles, Hodges recruited a stalwart band of character actors with plenty of experience, particularly in television. Godfrey Quigley (Eddie) and Kevin Brennan (Harry) had both made their first screen appearances in 1949, and had worked with Ian Hendry on *The Avengers*. Brennan went on to enjoy a second career behind the scenes as a gaffer and horror make-up specialist. Liz McKenzie (Mrs Brumby) and Geraldine Sherman (Albert's girlfriend) had both worked with Ken Loach in *Cathy Come Home* and *Poor Cow* respectively. John Hussey (Architect) had played Sir Miles Bishton in *The Reckoning*, and Ben Aris's (Interior Designer) credits included *If* (Lindsay Anderson, 1968), *The Charge of the Light Brigade* (Tony Richardson, 1968) and the part of Rosencrantz in Tony Richardson's *Hamlet* (1969). Appropriately, however, the mystery man remains Carl Howard, who played

Carter's assassin: *Get Carter* appears to be his only film appearance. Hodges, however, has shed some light on the mystery:

> Carl was an extra – a pallbearer – in my 1969 TV film *Rumour*. I gave him a line and the wrong extra was credited. I promised I'd make it up to him, and did. Except that he got left off the credits in the first prints of *Carter*. Meanwhile *Rumour* was repeated and we made sure the *Radio Times* and *TV Times* got it right. Unfortunately they trimmed the listings and both omitted him! Carl and credits didn't seem destined for each other.[67]

SHOOTING *CARTER*

'Will all members of the unit please take plenty of warm clothes to Newcastle, as the weather is very much colder there than in the London area.' Derek Gibson, *Carter* location manager, *Movement Order*, 21 July 1970, MGM British Studios

Bryan Mosley once remarked that 'The sun doesn't shine once in *Get Carter*',[68] and to look at Michael Caine in his black raincoat striding grimly beneath leaden skies, it would be easy to believe that the film was shot in the depths of winter. In fact, location filming in the north east took place between late July and mid-September, but photographs of the production crew suggest that the weather was closer to December. A photograph of filming on the funeral scene published in *Kinematograph Weekly* on 23 August 1970 shows everyone well wrapped up in waterproofs and fur-trimmed parkas. Five weeks earlier, it had all been a lot more glamorous when the same publication covered the film's launch party hosted by MGM's Robert Littman.[69] The film went into production under the working title *Carter*, and this title also appeared on the first paperback publication of Lewis's novel (Pan Books, 1971), produced to tie in with the movie's release. Before leaving for Newcastle on 21 July, Hodges spent an uncomfortable day at his prop man's house filming the faux porno movie that his protagonist would later view in a Tyneside tower block. He also shot all the scenes involving Britt Ekland, John Bindon and Terence Rigby, some of which (including a scene showing the disfiguration of Ekland's face at the hands of Rigby's character) would not survive the film's final cut. Ekland, Bindon and Rigby would not be required in Newcastle and, in fact, Caine was the only actor to take the train north with the production crew.

Determined that his location work should capture the authentic flavour of Tyneside, Hodges paid enormous attention to detail, carefully casting his extras and employing the real people associated with the locations whenever possible. Hence, the women who fight each other in a nightclub fracas were genuine antagonists in real life, and many of the guests at Kinnear's orgy had attended similar parties in the house in which it was filmed. MGM estimated that the film had employed about 1,500 extras.[70] As a devotee of Fellini's cinema, Hodges was keen to enliven his crowd scenes by finding extras with interesting faces. He quickly discovered that he did not have to look too far. 'Newcastle was filled with amazing Hogarthian faces,' he later recalled.[71]

As a group of outsiders from the south arriving with a star actor closely associated with London lad culture to make a film with Geordie 'colour', the film unit was conscious of the potential for friction with local sensibilities. They knew they were walking on eggshells when, early in the shooting schedule, the unit was filming in the Scotswood Road area of the city. Hodges had chosen to show Frank Carter's funeral cortège leaving from the back of a row of terraces because many of the fronts were boarded up awaiting demolition. Some local residents were scandalised by what they considered an insulting portrayal of northern funeral customs. One woman castigated the director, telling him in no uncertain terms that 'I don't care what you do down London, but up here we don't take hearses down back lanes.'[72] It was a timely reminder of the bitterness that marked Britain's north/south divide, and of the need to mobilise local support for the movie. On the first day of shooting, a diplomatic Michael Caine had told Newcastle's *Evening Chronicle* that, although he had not had much time to look around on his first visit to the city, he was already very impressed with its people, adding, 'The women are wearing the same clothes as they are in London and it's the least provincial of all the towns I've been to.'[73] On returning to London, however, the account he gave to his Geordie friend Ian La Frenais was rather more typically metropolitan: 'I've always gone on about this working-class image I've got and so on; but now I've been to Newcastle I realize I'm middle-class.'[74] Two decades later, Caine recalled his first impressions of Tyneside in his autobiography:

> By now I had seen poverty in different parts of the world that had made my own childhood look quite privileged, but I had never witnessed misery like this in my own country; it was Charles Dickens meets Emily Brontë, written by Edgar Wallace. Being in the far north of England, the weather was also dark and foreboding, the perfect atmosphere for our movie.[75]

Michael Klinger, too, had been quite shocked by the toughness of the culture he found on Tyneside. By way of illustration, he recalled the occasion during the shoot in the Scotswood Road area when Caine had been approached by one of the urchins who hung around the production unit. The kid had presented the star with a piece of toilet paper to sign. When Caine obliged with his autograph, the boy had looked at it, inquired about the name, declared that he had never heard of it, and ripped up the paper.[76] On another occasion when Caine was signing autographs, a girl had told him candidly, 'Me mum said you were good-looking. But I think y'er ugly.'[77]

Also aware of the controversial nature of the film's subject matter, and the local hornets' nest stirred up in similar circumstances by the filming of *Brighton Rock*, a spokesperson for the *Carter* film unit had assured the *Chronicle* that this most location-specific of movies was to be set in an anonymous city in the north, and that it was 'extremely doubtful if many will recognize it as Newcastle'.[78] A positive relationship with the city was further promoted two nights later when MGM hosted a cocktail party in the Royal Station Hotel, opposite the bar used as a location on the first day of filming, and the base for the production.[79] Like Caine, the film's producers tried not to miss a trick in the public relations department, also showering Newcastle's womenfolk with compliments and declaring them 'the prettiest girls' in England.[80] The policy of flattery, largesse, good humour and the employment of local extras paid dividends, and towards the end of his eight-week stay in the north east, producer Michael Klinger felt confident enough to abandon earlier caution and emphasise his film's connection with the area:

> We love the dramatic way in which the old is mixed with the new in Newcastle. We love the river bridges, the way in which the city is built on different levels. And the people ... they are incredibly nice without being phoney. Newcastle will be one of the stars of the [film] ... as much a part of the action as Paris in *Rififi*, San Francisco in *Bullitt*, Los Angeles in *Harper*.[81]

When Ian Hendry arrived in Newcastle in August, the film's director and producer were immediately conscious of his alcohol problem and the animosity towards Michael Caine that his drinking exacerbated. As Hendry got stuck in to some serious drinking on the night before his first scene, it became evident to all that he was deeply jealous of Caine's success. It was a situation that could easily have lowered morale and created tensions in the entire production unit, but Caine and Hodges were canny enough to channel Hendry's negativity and use it to give an extra edge to the encounters between Carter and Eric.

Location work in Newcastle and Gateshead occupied about four weeks of the film's shooting schedule before the unit moved on to Hamsterley, County Durham, to film the scenes at Kinnear's mansion, and Blackhall Rocks on the Durham coast for the film's final sequence. By early September, the unit was back on Tyneside to complete the shooting schedule, finally filming parts of the titles sequence during their return to London on 17 September. Writer Ted Lewis attended the early filming, approving Hodges' changes to his novel and declaring himself particularly impressed with Caine's portrayal of the character he had created: 'He's ideal casting for the part, and I can't really imagine any other actor doing it as well.'[82]

By the time Hodges returned to London, he had all the footage to assemble *Get Carter*, but one vital ingredient was missing: music. Michael Klinger, however, knew just the man for the job: Roy Budd. Hodges had seen Budd play jazz piano a number of times, but had not thought of him as a film composer. But when he heard Budd's ideas for the score, he was immediately struck by a few plaintive chords embedded in the title music and realised that they would make a dramatically simple theme for key passages in the picture.[83] Budd's harpsichord theme has become as evocative of the atmosphere of *Get Carter* as Anton Karas's zither tune is of *The Third Man* (Carol Reed, 1949).

Already a highly respected jazz musician, Budd was just twenty-three years old when he composed *Get Carter*. It was only his second film score,[84] and he accepted the commission on the tiny budget of £450, working with the other two members of his jazz trio, Jeff Clyne (bass) and Chris Karan (percussion). Influenced by the innovative scores of Ennio Morricone, Budd approached the sessions at the Olympic Studios, Barnes in a spirit of experimentation. Both diegetic and non-diegetic music was required, and for the snatches of rock music heard in the Long Bar and at Kinnear's party, Budd turned to the lyric-writing talent of his manager Jack Fishman. It is Budd's haunting theme and incidental music with its bizarre instrumentation, however, that lives in the memory. It combines harpsichord, electric piano, double bass and tablas (courtesy of the percussionist's time in India).[85] The composer went on to work on over fifty film scores before his death at only forty-six in 1993.

CARTER IN CONTEXT

High Risers

'There's nothing so holy but money will corrupt and putrefy it. [...]
You are happy in England, my lord; here they sell justice with those
weights that they press men to death with.' Flamineo in John Webster,
The White Devil, III.iii.24–5, 27–8

On 13 August 1970, midway through the filming of *Get Carter*, the north
east was rocked by a four-second earth tremor, causing particular distress
to residents of tower blocks. This was hardly surprising, given that the
disastrous collapse of a similar block at Ronan Point was a recent
memory. In hindsight, it is easy to see this ominous rumble as a portent
of the scandals that would shake the north east in the early 1970s.

For the previous ten years, Tyneside had been at the centre of the
modernist project, which transformed Britain's urban landscape in the
post-war years. The twin principles of town planning and slum clearance, applied in the aftermath of Nazi bombing, ripped apart the historic
centres of many British towns and cities, replacing roads with urban
motorways and flyovers, streets with shopping precincts and terrace
houses with high-rise blocks of flats. On Tyneside, the architect of
change was the leader of Newcastle Council, the Labour radical T. Dan
Smith – known to his admirers as 'Mr Newcastle'. A firm advocate of
the independence of the local state, Smith was a visionary who believed
that, with the wholesale application of modern planning and building
techniques, his city could rival 'Venice, Athens, Florence and Rome' as
a European cultural centre.[86] To this end, he brought in the town planning and social engineering guru Wilf Burns in 1963.

Burns was not a man to allow local customs, mores and sentiments
to dilute his modernist precepts. He believed he knew what was best for
people and they had better accept his brave new world. Paradoxically,
his ultra-modern version of social engineering now looks suspiciously
like Victorian conceptions of the disciplinary society:

In a huge city, it is a fairly common observation that the dwellers in
a slum are almost a separate race of people with different values,
aspirations and ways of living. One result of slum clearance is that a
considerable movement of people takes place over long distances with
a devastating effect on the social groupings built up over the years. But,
one might argue, this is a good thing when we are dealing with people

who have no initiative or civic pride. The task, surely, is to break up such groupings, even though the people seem to be satisfied with their miserable environment and seem to enjoy an extrovert social life in their locality.[87]

With the devastation of the north east's industrial infrastructure still in the future, the physical reconstruction of Tyneside blazed ahead, creating unprecedented opportunities for poorly remunerated local politicians to supplement their income in illicit ways, as the campaigning Labour MP Tom Milne made clear:

> Apart from a sense of importance and self-aggrandisement, MPs and Councillors could easily pick up paid directorships, fees and expenses, both from public enterprises and from companies in the private sector contracting for public works, roads, hospitals, schools and housing schemes. One could be a Labour Councillor voting on public expenditure for these schemes and, at the same time, a private contractor making extremely good profits out of the contract. The safe Labour majorities made the positions of both MPs and Councillors secure.[88]

It was T. Dan Smith who set the standards in north-eastern public life at the time. The Trotskyist politician seemed to see no contradiction in the fact that he was also a public relations consultant for the Crudens building company who won lucrative contracts for blocks of flats from the council, the Peterlee Development Corporation, and for the Labour Party. The role of Dan Smith as a power broker in the north east meant that most local MPs were protective of him. In 1962, Smith was hired as a public relations consultant by the Leeds architect John Poulson, whose practice was closely aligned with the construction firms Bovis Holdings, the family company of the then Conservative Minister of Housing, Keith Joseph, and Marples Ridgeway, a firm predominantly owned by the Transport Minister, Ernest Marples. Smith also had a close working relationship with the corrupt County Durham alderman, Andrew Cunningham, whose many public roles included chair of the Northumbrian River Authority and Durham Police Authority, and membership of the Labour Party National Executive Committee. Smith introduced Cunningham to Poulson in 1963. It was a system of mutual benefit that bridged radical political divisions and ensured that any close inspection of its undertakings was effectively discouraged. As Milne puts it, 'There were plenty of officials and councillors around willing to be bought, and more important, many in high places who were willing

5. *Dryderdale Hall, the home of Vince Landa and Cyril Kinnear.*

and able to foster these activities whilst themselves remaining in the background, but being helpful in any cover-up operations that were required.'[89] One of those implicated in Milne's accusation was Reginald Maudling, the Tory Home Secretary at the time of the inquiry into Poulson's affairs and a director of his company.

Poulson quickly secured contracts all over the north east. The invulnerability of the venal system of local government contracting seemed to be confirmed by Dan Smith's appointment as chair of the Northern Economic Planning Council and to the Royal Commission on Local Government in 1966. Before the end of 1969, however, the greed of council officials was to prove Poulson's undoing. So many sweeteners had been paid that his architectural practice was declared insolvent. It was only a matter of time until the shit hit the fan.

As the script for *Get Carter* was being written, intimations of corrupt local government practices were at last beginning to surface in the north-eastern press, but the full implications would not be revealed until after the film's release when Poulson, Cunningham and Smith would all receive gaol sentences. The venality of these men did not, however, prevent them from believing that they had made a genuine contribution to the economic regeneration of the north. As T. Dan Smith whinged after his conviction:

For all the work I have done for the community, for all the early promise of distinction and power, I am left with nothing [...] People like me are expected to work full-time without salaries, without staff, or even postage stamps. I for one couldn't afford such a situation. And that is where Poulson filled the gap [...] I came to the conclusion that I was missing out, that I could combine my real desire to give public service with what they call a piece of the action.[90]

By the mid-1970s, the prisons of England were to become melting pots for the corrupt representatives of many walks of life, as local government officials and their contractors joined senior policemen and gang bosses in a disturbing fellowship of crime.

High Rollers and Heavy Rollers

> 'Princes give rewards with their own hands
> But death and punishment by the hands of others.'
>
> Gasparo, in John Webster, *The White Devil*, V.vi.191–2

The well-publicised trials and convictions of the London gangs run by the Kray and Richardson brothers had, by the end of the 1960s, rekindled the commercial potential of the gangster film in Britain. Although the Great Train Robbery of 1963 had inspired one notable film – *Robbery* (Peter Yates, 1967) – the genre had become unfashionable as the upbeat mood accompanying 'Swinging London' switched the attention of film-makers towards lighter subjects with greater international appeal. The major backers of British film-making at the time were the Hollywood studios and, as far as they were concerned, crime subjects were best treated in a spectacular (James Bond) or comedic (Ealing) fashion. Their preferred solution was the caper film, a sub-genre that seemed to capture the frivolousness and irreverence of the era. Michael Caine had already starred in a number of capers, including *Gambit* (Ronald Neame, 1966) and *The Italian Job*. But with the arrest of the Krays, the spotlight was suddenly illuminating the darker recesses of the criminal underworld. There was a realisation that British criminals might now be convincingly depicted as being as tough and ruthless as their American counterparts. A sensitive observer like Mike Hodges quickly appreciated the need to revise the customary representation of the British gangster:

> British criminals never did anything we saw people do in American film noir; nothing really unpleasant or sadistic. Then it all changed with the

Krays and the Richardsons trials. Suddenly one realized there was a whole other game going on. And it wasn't just in London. There was a killing in Newcastle in a nightclub called La Dolce Vita, for example.[91]

Although the murder took place after a visit to La Dolce Vita rather than on its premises, the name of the club with its connotations of style and hedonism perfectly captured the transformation that took place in Tyneside's nightlife after the Betting and Gaming Act of 1960. Previously, 'clubland' in the north-east context had meant the 1,500 working men's clubs where the toilers in the area's heavy industries could refresh themselves with local brown ale and watch a modest cabaret. But as improving wage levels and permissive legislation came together in the early 1960s, a new gloss was given to the entertainment business. The working men's clubs were stocked with newly legal 'one-armed bandit' slot machines, and the underground gambling dens surfaced as exotic casinos on the American and continental models. With its work hard/play hard tradition, Newcastle became the Las Vegas of the north. A new breed of entertainment entrepreneurs, often with criminal links, emerged. Together with those reaping fat profits from the architectural transformation of northern cities, they lived an ostentatious lifestyle, stirring contradictory emotions of envy and disgust among ordinary Geordies. Some of these clubland cavaliers moved north from London, where the voracious demands of protection racketeers were inhibiting business expansion. The north-east gold rush would quickly be slowed by the erosion of the area's economic infrastructure, but for a decade it roared ahead, drawing in claim jumpers as well as prospectors, and redrawing the map of Tyneside's underworld.

In *Get Carter*, the profiteers of the new leisure culture are represented by fruit machine distributor Cliff Brumby and the 'governor' of Tyneside, Cyril Kinnear, who has a business arrangement with the powerful London mobsters, the Fletcher brothers. Kinnear supplies pornography for the Fletchers to distribute. In return, they supply Kinnear with back-up enforcement services and the insurance supplied by their reputation in the criminal community. This symbiotic relationship has been forged by the hospitality offered by Kinnear during a visit from the Fletchers. There are striking parallels with the *modus operandi* of the Kray brothers.

By 1963, having established their power base in the East End of London, the Krays were looking to extend their business nationally and internationally. They took over two clubs in Birmingham and one in Leicester, and they negotiated a reciprocal agreement with a leading

Glasgow mobster who supplied a gunman for one of the Krays' 'hits' in London.[92] The twins were also courting American Mafia contacts, and were impressed with their practice of importing hitmen from other cities to carry out murders. They first developed an interest in Newcastle when their showbiz friend, the American singer Billy Daniels, was booked to appear at the city's La Dolce Vita Club in 1964. Fellow villain Eric Mason arranged hospitality from the club's owners, David Marcus and Norman Levy. The Levys sent two Rolls-Royces to meet the seven-strong Kray party at Newcastle station. 'As the evening progressed,' recalled Mason, 'we met the guys who ran things in Newcastle.'[93] Among those introduced to the twins was the playboy Angus Sibbet, an operative of the slot machine and nightclub magnate Vincent Landa. Another of Landa's employees, the flamboyant East Ender Dennis Stafford, was already known to the Krays as someone who had crossed them as a juvenile.[94] In 1967, Stafford, together with Landa's brother Michael Lavaglio, would be convicted of Sibbet's murder. The conviction, however, was one of the most unsafe in recent memory.

After meeting the men who ran Newcastle, it seems that the Kray twins, who already profited from slot machines in London's West End, decided that they would like a 'slice of the action' in the north. In the summer of 1966, they returned to La Dolce Vita with the legendary boxer, Joe Louis, for whom they had fixed up a series of personal appearances in northern clubs. Their relationship with the Levys was firmly cemented. Acknowledging the £5,000 donated by the Levys towards the twins' defence fund after their arrest, Ronnie Kray later described them as 'good friends at a time when good friends were hard to find'.[95] The Krays also paid a visit to Landa's flagship gambling club, the Piccadilly, which was managed by Stafford. They were shown round by Sibbet's minder. Soon afterwards, Landa's business empire came under sustained attack. When offers of 'protection' were declined, three premises were burned down, including the Piccadilly Club.[96] Whether or not the Krays played any part in Sibbet's murder remains a matter of conjecture. Sibbet was known to be embezzling substantial sums from the takings of his employer's machines, and paying sweeteners to club stewards, and this may have supplied a motive for his killing. Certainly, the case raised considerable doubts about the probity and impartiality of a Durham Constabulary which rushed to judgement on Dennis Stafford, a petty criminal whose *chutzpah* had frequently left the police and prison services with egg on their faces. The mysterious death of Vince Landa's bad lieutenant shed a dark light on the murky world of the north east's gangland, suggesting much more about its internal and external connections than it confirmed. Hodges researched the case carefully in his preparations for his film, and emphasised its relevance by using Landa's hastily vacated country house as the location for Kinnear's home. The house was within the jurisdiction of the County Durham Police Authority which, under the chairmanship of Cunningham was, one might say, rotten from the top down.

Rollers

'A black and white roller used to cost us two and a half quid. It sold for anything from £10 to £15. Colour rollers: the 200 foot was a fiver, that started at £25, and the 400 foot, which was two films in one, the sky was the limit.' Derek Cox, porn shop manager in 1960s Soho[97]

At the beginning of 1971, shortly before *Get Carter*'s release, police at Grimsby docks discovered 1,300 reels of pornographic film (known in the trade as 'rollers') and ninety-six sets of obscene colour slides in a cargo of animal offal.[98] Grimsby is a stone's throw from Lewis's original setting for his story. The late 1960s and early 1970s were growth years for the porn trade. What had been a small underground cottage industry was transformed by changes in public attitudes, substantial increases in supply and, in London, the corrupt practices of that squad of police officers charged with the control of obscene publications. Soho had long been the centre of the trade in Britain, and from the mid-1950s it was dominated by a syndicate controlled by the vice barons Bernie Silver and Frank Mifsud. By the time Lewis was writing his book about the supply of films to the trade, they had been joined by two other major players: John Mason and Jimmy Humphries. Their businesses were effectively licensed and protected by an elaborate system of illicit payments to the Metropolitan Police's Obscene Publications Squad (OPS) and their senior controllers at West End Central and Scotland Yard.[99] By 1970 the number of shops in Soho selling erotic materials had grown to over forty, most of them dealing (via their back rooms) in hard-core magazines and films imported from Scandinavia and the USA.[100]

The presentation of the erotic on screen is as old as cinema itself, but before the late 1950s, the exhibition of 'blue' films was a strictly clandestine affair in Britain. It was a question of knowing someone who might know a man who could arrange a private screening at a stag party or similar single-sex gathering. The films were invariably foreign, usually French or American in origin. What changed this situation was as much an advancement in technology as a loosening of moral prohibitions. The availability of affordable 8mm cameras and film projectors for domestic use opened up new opportunities for producers of 'glamour' magazines like the photographer George Harrison Marks. In 1958, he began to produce and distribute three-minute soft-core reels featuring his models in states of undress. His challenge was quickly taken up by competitors such as Stanley Long and Peter Walker, and the films began to get longer and more elaborate as business boomed in the early 1960s. One of these films, *Soho Striptease* (Roger Proudlock, 1960) featured the performers from Michael Klinger's Gargoyle Club, and first introduced the future producer of *Get Carter* to the possibilities of film-making.[101]

As competition in the 8mm glamour film business intensified, one or two producers decided to chance their arms with stronger fare. Unlike the products of Marks, Long and Walker, which were on discreet but open sale at legitimate retailers and via mail order, the work of underground hard-core film-makers Mike Freeman and Ivor Cooke was confined to the back rooms of Soho sex shops. The films began as silent reels in monochrome, but by the end of the 1960s, they had been upgraded to colour and sound. Freeman, however, had little opportunity to take advantage of technological improvements. He was sentenced to eighteen months' imprisonment on obscenity charges in 1966, and not too long after his release was back inside on a life sentence, having killed a man he claimed was a hitman sent to carry out an underworld contract on him.[102] The vacuum left by Freeman was quickly filled by the shameless John Lindsay, a Scottish photographer who began to shoot blue films around 1969, at the start of the extension of the pornography business to new markets. Happy to publicise his activities, Lindsay allowed one of his filming sessions to be recorded by Stanley Long for his documentary *Naughty* (1971). His brazenness may have had something to do with the protection afforded by the systematic bribes he was paying to the OPS. The session was filmed at about the time of *Get Carter*'s release, and the title of the resulting blue movie, *Sex After School*, echoed the name given to the faux stag film that Carter sees in Newcastle, *Teacher's Pet*. Although Lindsay used adult performers, he liked to give the impression that they were younger, even at one time filming in a genuine school (with the connivance of the caretaker and head boy).[103] Although there is no contemporary evidence of the production of hardcore films in the north of England, the nearest real-life equivalent to *Get Carter*'s Cyril Kinnear was a home counties pornographer called 'Big

Jeff' Phillips. His main business in the early 1970s was the importation of Danish porn films for the Soho market, but he also made some of his own. Shortly before committing suicide in 1975 he described his entry into film-making to the *Sunday Mirror*:

> I started from nothing ten years ago and soon made a fortune. It was easy – I got a good movie camera, hired men and girls from the coffee bars and pubs around Soho for a fiver or a tenner a time and made the films in flats or houses borrowed from friends. They were filthy of course but technically very good. I sold them myself at first for £100 or £200 a copy. Then I was 'sent for' by a big dealer in porn [...] who persuaded me to deal only through him. [...] I could get £1,000 a copy for my movies through him. He also arranged introductions to detectives who named their price for leaving my business alone.[104]

Phillips was able to buy himself a white Rolls-Royce, two blocks of flats, houses in Esher and Kingston, and a mansion in the Berkshire countryside. The mansion, which the *Sunday People* exposed as 'the stately home paid for with filth', was called 'High Crockett'.[105] Kinnear's country seat was named 'The Heights'.

But although *Get Carter* is ostensibly about the blue film racket, the corruption of Doreen by pornographers is also a metaphor for a much more general malaise affecting urban Britain at the end of the 1960s. Hodges remains in no doubt that the scandals of the era were interconnected. He knew, for example, from the scandals that had rocked first the Sheffield and then the Leeds Constabulary shortly before *Get Carter* that police impropriety was not confined to London: 'I had worked on *World in Action*, so I knew there were whole strata of the police force which were corrupt. You sensed that *Carter* wasn't just about pornographic films – it extended to local councils and building controls, undercurrents which eventually proved true with T. Dan Smith and Poulson.'[106] Hodges never makes these connections as explicit as Lewis does in his novel, but they none the less ground the narrative implicitly in the secret sub-world of the local state. Beneath the dramatic surface of *Get Carter* lies a network that links un-civil servants, jerry builders and the cash to be made from bent coppers, squandered sixpences and pounds of porn.

TWO
From London Luxury to Terminal Beach

PRE-CREDITS SEQUENCE

'In the beginning is the end but we still go on.' Samuel Beckett, *Waiting for Godot*

From a godlike vantage point, we see Carter framed theatrically in the window of the Fletcher brothers' penthouse apartment. 'I wanted to be up high so I could make it appear like a dream,' Hodges remarked in his commentary on the DVD release of the film. The lighting gives Caine an ethereal quality that makes it seem as if he is already 'up in heaven'. Hodges gives his first clue to the end of his film as the image of his protagonist is wiped away by the closing curtains. The pre-production version of the scene stressed the seediness rather than the glamour of criminal life in London, with Carter seen through the rain-lashed window of a decaying Victorian pile that sounds as if it should be in *The Ladykillers* (Alexander MacKendrick, 1955).[1]

The screen is suddenly flooded by ethereal light, but ironically it turns out to be projecting pornographic images on a screen in the apartment. The audience includes Carter, the Fletchers (London mobsters loosely modelled on the Kray twins) and Gerald Fletcher's wife, Anna. Hodges had once been shown locally produced photographs like these by a props man when they had worked for Granada Television in Manchester, and the dialogue makes it clear that this porn, too, originates in the north of England where the Fletchers have 'connections'. It is also clear that Carter's employers are unhappy about his investigation into his brother's recent death. The apparent cause of that death is subtly evoked when Carter picks up a whisky decanter.

The scene sets up a number of contrasts that will be significant in the film. First, it establishes the lifestyle that Carter enjoys as a privileged member of the Fletchers' firm, which will be seen to be very different from his humble origins in Newcastle. Second, it draws attention to the differences between Carter and the Fletchers. These are centred not only on the issues of Jack's attachment to his brother and to Anna, but in the temperamental contrasts clear in the scene. These oppositions are suggested in the way in which Carter and Gerald Fletcher are seated apart, on different sides of the room. Finally, the scene hints at the moral dilemma that preoccupies Carter: his professional duty as an employee versus his personal code of honour.

Studio executives at MGM in Hollywood were concerned about the dialogue in the scene, and decided to amend it and to revoice Terence Rigby and John Bindon (who play the Fletchers), making the opening more intelligible for American audiences. 'Bollock naked' became 'bare-arsed naked'. 'We have connections in those parts', was explicated as, 'you know we're connected with the Newcastle mob'. The idiomatic 'bugle' in 'they won't take kindly to someone from London poking his bugle in', was altered to 'nose', adding 'remember they're killers just like you'. Gerald's line, 'I smell trouble, boy' was deleted, and Sid Fletcher's 'The law was satisfied' was changed to 'The police seemed satisfied'.[2] Hodges was far from satisfied with the 'improvements', and insisted that British prints should carry the original dialogue and voices.

TITLE SEQUENCE

'I see now there's nothing sure in mortality but mortality.' Vindice in Thomas Middleton or Cyril Tourneur, *The Revenger's Tragedy*, III.vi.89

Memorable as the sequence that accompanies Roy Budd's celebrated theme tune, the titles and credits cover Carter's train journey from London to Newcastle. The journey is, however, far from being merely a convenient and scenic backdrop for the title graphics. Filmed on location, mostly with a hand-held camera giving a sense of immediacy, the sequence is packed with detailed information. We are shown Carter's (guilty?) obsessiveness in his fastidious attention to cleanliness and his health, as he cleans a spoon, administers nose drops, and pops a pill. The fastidiousness is reflected in his well-cut suit and crisp white shirt, and helps to establish his difference. Like the Jacobean figure of the malcontent, Carter is a socially marginal character, a displaced person, his social and geographical mobility suggested by the train journey he takes. As they are in *Brighton Rock* (1948), newspaper headlines are used casually to indicate the dangers awaiting him: the violent gangland feud that will underpin the film's action. Finally, and crucially, Hodges gives further intimations of Carter's mortality. First, his protagonist reads *Farewell My Lovely*, not only an omen of his demise, but a homage to Ted Lewis's favourite author: Raymond Chandler. Second, Hodges actually shows the man who will later turn out to be Carter's nemesis sitting in the opposite corner of the carriage and wearing a signet ring engraved with the letter 'J'.[3] The trope of the identifying ring was probably inspired by the 'E' signet Eric wears in Lewis's book and is the last thing Carter sees as Eric takes aim with the shotgun. But the circular character of the ring also serves as an apt way of symbolising the cycle of life and death, the 'return home'.[4]

A further homage to *Brighton Rock* was left on the cutting-room floor. The first day of shooting included a scene in which Carter, on arrival at the central station, is spotted by an *Evening Chronicle* seller who, together with the station taxi controller, is in the pay of the gang who murdered Frank.[5] A newspaper employee and surveillance at a railway terminus clearly recall the opening scenes of the Boulting brothers' film.

THE LONG BAR

'Hardness becomes the visage of a man well:
It argues service, resolution, manhood ... '

Beatrice in Thomas Middleton and William Rowley,
The Changeling (1612), II.ii.94–5

On arrival in Newcastle, Carter goes to a pub near the station to meet Margaret, his brother's last sexual partner, but receives a phone call telling him that she cannot keep the appointment. The scene is notable for its unusual combination of documentary realism and star promotion. Editor John Trumper cuts between the faces of the suspicious locals in the pub and the figure of Michael Caine, famously ordering a pint of bitter 'in a thin glass' and speaking to Margaret on the telephone.[6] Wolfgang Suschitzky films the locals in a way that emphasises their bizarreness and their difference from Carter's adopted metropolitan persona, even picking out one character with an extra finger on his hand. It was Caine's screen presence, however, that made the biggest impression on his director. It was the first time that Hodges had worked with a genuine film star:

I was looking through the camera when he's called to the phone, walks the length of the bar, and fills the screen. I realised that I was in a completely different ball game. It wasn't to do with reality any longer, it was something else I had no idea of [...] and that changed my whole conception of film-making.[7]

From that moment, Suschitzky was obliged to combine his *cinéma vérité* style with the careful lighting of Caine's face to bring out the cold and calculating nature of his character.

The scene was filmed in the North Eastern public house adjacent to the central station. The locals were given £5 a head and MGM footed the drinks bill.[8] Not surprisingly, the availability of free booze prolonged the length of the shoot, with more than one extra having to be helped out of the pub. In line with Hodges' social realist policy, one of the North Eastern's actual barmen, John Cavanagh, was asked to play himself and to deliver the line 'Is there a Mr Carter in the house?' He pocketed a fee of £105, the best part of a month's wages for a barman at the time.[9] A sequence in which Carter hires a car and drives to his boarding house was dropped from the film's final cut.[10] Instead, Carter goes directly to his family home.

JACK'S RETURN HOME

There seemed to be a great deal of Gateshead and the whole town appeared to have been carefully planned by an enemy of the human race in its more exuberant aspects. Insects can do better than this: their habitations are equally monotonous but far more efficiently constructed. [...] The town was built to work in and sleep in. You can still sleep in it, I suppose. J. B. Priestley, *English Journey* (1933), London: Mandarin, 1994, p. 301

Carter goes to pay his respects to his brother, who is laid out in his coffin in the living room of the family home. Hodges economically conveys both the constancy of the world Carter has left and his enduring memories of it, by having him locate the latchkey in its accustomed hiding place behind the letterbox. The means of entrance to his childhood home puts him back in touch with his past and a culture of trust he no longer shares. Filmed in a condemned terrace house in (the appropriately named) Frank Street in Benwell, the scenes that follow eschew the type of nostalgic romanticism of the old back-to-backs favoured by scholarship boys like Richard Hoggart. Instead, Hodges and Suschitzky use their documentary experience to exploit the cramped filming conditions and sparse light to evoke the profound drabness of urban life in the less privileged quarters of the provinces. Although production designer Assheton Gorton must have contributed to the refurbishing of the derelict house, the interiors look entirely naturalistic. It is hard to believe that we are viewing the work of the same designer who gave *The Knack* its op art feel and created the modernist interiors for *Blow-up* and the psychedelic dreamscapes for *Wonderwall*.

As Caine moves through the house, he visibly registers its continuities and changes, its state of decay. Frank is dead, and the house, with all its cultural and personal resonances, is dying, fading to the colour of earth. When he reaches his brother's bedroom he is reminded that he no longer enjoys the anonymity afforded by London. As he peers through the net curtains at the Land Rover cruising past his door, he knows he is back in a culture of surveillance where nobody's business is their own. His thoughts turn to the shotgun that Lewis tells us represents the childhood bond between Jack and Frank, who had made clandestine hunting trips together into the country. He is reassured that it is exactly where he expected to find it. As the weapon of a hunter, it symbolises Carter's mission, but it carries few of the connotations associated with his profession as an underworld enforcer. Unlike the pump-action version featured in the film's publicity photographs or the sniper's rifle that ends Carter's life, the long-barrelled shotgun is an unsophisticated rural weapon, lacking in precision and reliability. Carter never actually fires it, and in Lewis's book it fails at the crucial moment. It is Frank's weapon rather than Jack's, and Jack carries it as an emblem of the wrong he has come to right. Above all, it is a family weapon. As Hodges comments: 'He didn't really like Frank, but Frank was family. The really important thing for Carter and his ilk is family. And this is based on a truth […] they're terribly sentimental, gangsters.'[11]

Be it truth or stereotype, urban criminal organisations have relied on the bonds of trust and loyalty nurtured by the institution of the family, and gangster fictions from Jacobean drama to *Jack's Return Home* had used those bonds to motivate their narratives of blood revenge. When Jack Carter views the remains of his brother (stoically played by Michael Klinger's chauffeur, Reg Niven) he knows that this attack on his extended self cannot go unpunished. Enhanced by Budd's poignant musical phrase, Caine's restrained performance here relies on his audience's own family ties: 'When I see my dead brother, I just stand there and take it in. The audience adds it all for you. If it was their brother, how would they feel? They're doing all the emoting for you.'[12]

Carter breaks his vigil at his brother's coffin to book a room at the knowingly named Las Vegas Guest House, a slightly larger terrace house in Coburg Street, Gateshead, that the blowsy landlady refers to as 'the hotel'. The name evokes Newcastle's role as the bright lights gaming playground of the north. The garish neon sign in the window simultaneously pokes fun at the pretensions of its proprietor and recalls the films Hodges had made for *World in Action* in America.[13] The conversation between Carter and Edna the Landlady is laced with sexual innuendo that hints at the bawdy sub-world beneath the veneer of working-class respectability.

THE FUNERAL

'On our way back from Hebburn to Gateshead, which was a journey among the very scrag-ends of industrial life, we passed no less than three funerals, each of them with a long black tail to it. Here, though you can no longer live well, you can still be buried in style. [...] There were flowers for the dead, if none for the living.' J. B. Priestley, *English Journey*, pp. 318–19

On the morning of the funeral, Carter shaves above the body of his brother. Some might recall the disturbing notion that hair on a corpse continues to grow, but the ritual of hair-cutting, as an act of purification, is a common one in those dedicating their life to revenge or setting out on a mission of sanitation. The classic example in cinema is the shaven head of Travis Bickle in *Taxi Driver* (Martin Scorsese, 1976). As the funeral party gathers, Carter comes face to face with Doreen, the sixteen-year-old who has been raised as Frank's daughter, but who (as Lewis's novel makes clear) might easily be Jack's offspring. Her parentage was a major source of friction between the Carter brothers, and her presence is a constant reminder of the guilt that – although unacknowledged – partly fuels Jack's drive for revenge. Their awkward exchanges are punctuated by shots of the screws being noisily inserted into the lid of Frank's coffin. These macabre twists emphasise the grimness of the situation and contrast with Carter's glib offer to take Doreen to South America with his 'fiancée'. Hodges had begun his film-making career in television with a documentary on funeral directors called *The British Way of Death* (1963), and he puts his knowledge of the details of undertaking to good use, giving the funeral procedures an unimpeachable feeling of authenticity.[14]

6. *'Piss-holes in the snow'. Michael Caine and Ian Hendry.*

As the hearse moves off to the crematorium in West Street, shadowed by the mysterious Land Rover, we glimpse what is now a lost Gateshead and Newcastle – serried rows of crumbling back-to-backs sloping down to Scotswood Road and the Tyne and the smoking chimneys beyond. If the funeral is Frank's, the elegy is equally for the old city and the passing of an era. In a city structured by inequality, however, class distinctions persist and Hodges takes the opportunity to contrast the modest Carter funeral with the more opulent procession leaving the crematorium. The solemnity of the committal service is broken by the entrance of Margaret, the clacking of her high heels signalling the disruptive presence of her sexuality in the narrative. Her status as a character with something to hide is clearly indicated by the sunglasses she wears and, less obviously, by the question mark created when the silver handle of her umbrella is held against her black coat. The scene ends with the flames licking round Frank's coffin, an anticipation of the violent conflagration to come.

In the wake scene at the Half Moon pub that follows, the simple platitudes of remembrance are in uneasy tension with the complexity of the underlying emotions and with Carter's need to progress with his murder investigation. Hodges brings out the painful irony of this counterpoint by fixing his camera on Petra Markham's Doreen, registering her mounting disquiet until she finally snaps and throws her Babycham over her father's friend, Eddie Appleyard. Carter, relying on the gangster's maxim that everything can be sorted by sweeteners or intimidation, quickly offers Eddie money for his dry-cleaning. Eddie is likely to be of little assistance in the search for Frank's killers, but Frank's workmate, Keith, is likely to be of more use. As a barman he has his ear to the ground, and can warn Carter about anyone on his tail. The pub used for this scene was the Victoria and Comet (jocularly known as the 'Spit and Vomit') on Neville Street close to production headquarters at the Royal Station Hotel. By 2002 it had become 'O'Neills'.[15]

In the shooting script, this scene is followed by a sequence that establishes Carter's adulterous relationship with Anna Fletcher. He phones her, but the presence of her husband makes it impossible to have the intimate conversation they desire.[16] Carter is then spotted by two gangsters and runs into a department store, where he avoids his pursuers by hiding in a photo booth. He emerges after posing for four police-identification-style photographs. The fifth is 'a close-up of a hand giving the "up you" sign'.[17]

THE RACECOURSE

'I'd fain get off, this man's not for my company,
I smell his brother's blood when I come near him.'

De Flores in Thomas Middleton and William Rowley,
The Changeling, IV.ii.40–41

Tipped off by Keith that he might find his old classmate Albert Swift there, Carter visits the local racecourse at Gosforth. But, although Albert is likely to be a mine of information on the Newcastle underworld, he has no desire to talk to Carter. When he spots Jack on the course he drops his hot dog in fear. Carter, however, is distracted by the sight of someone he had not expected to see: Eric Paice in a chauffeur's livery and dark glasses. Lewis's novel informs us that Carter had encountered Eric when he had worked for a rival mobster in London. The sarcasm that inflects their conversation suggests that there is no love lost between them, just as there was no love lost between the two actors. The racecourse scene was the first time they were together on screen. Hendry's drunken and resentful state had obliged Hodges to abandon an attempt to rehearse the scene in a hotel room on the night before, and when the two actors met on location at the racetrack there was what Hodges describes as a real 'edge' to the encounter. It cannot have helped that Hendry was now playing a chauffeur, a role that had propelled Caine to stardom in *Alfie*. The 'needle' reaches its sharpest when Caine removes Hendry's sunglasses and describes his eyes, disparagingly, as 'piss-holes in the snow'. 'It's a kind of threatening insult to take someone's glasses off,' Hodges has noted, because it is saying 'let's look in your real eyes and see your real soul'.[18]

The long lenses favoured by Hodges allow Suschitzky to situate the two men in the crowd of racegoers and to capture the detail and colour of the event. This technique of shooting 'stolen' footage during an unstaged event, as well as the choice of the racecourse as a location for the meeting of gangsters, may be regarded as further homage to Hodges' favourite British crime film, *Brighton Rock*.

THE HEIGHTS

'How shall I dare to venture in his castle
When he discharges murderers at the gate?
But I must go on, for back I cannot go.'

Alsemero in Thomas Middleton and William Rowley,
The Changeling, I.i.229–31

Carter trails Eric as he drives the high rollers back to the home of one of the local crime lords, Cyril Kinnear. The scenes at the ironically named 'The Heights' were shot at the hurriedly vacated country retreat of Vincent Landa, who had taken up residence in his villa in Majorca following the murder of Angus Sibbet. An ex-military policeman who, like Eric Paice, had a penchant for dark glasses, Landa had moved from London in the late 1950s and developed a highly lucrative business supplying amusement machines to clubland and booking variety acts. By the time of Sibbet's death, he held eleven company directorships, and was wealthy enough to own a white Rolls-Royce, a Pontiac Grand Prix and the £50,000, ten-roomed Dryderdale Hall near Hamsterley, County Durham, into which he had moved with his wife and six children from a council house in Peterlee.[19] Although, at the time, Michael Klinger and MGM's publicity spokesman dismissed the use of

the location as mere coincidence, Hodges was fully aware of the significance of the house and chose it deliberately.[20] It proved a perfect
location, wreaking of authenticity and full of useful details such as the
cowboys and indians wallpaper that Carter presses himself against as
he hides from Kinnear's bodyguards. A second ironic touch is the
African shield and crossed spears on the wall of the crime lord's living
room – a reminder of Caine's first major role in *Zulu* (Cy Endfield,
1963).

By evading Kinnear's guards and gatecrashing his gambling party
Carter is making the point that he is a professional, to be taken seriously.
His intrusion is a warning shot across Kinnear's bows. Kinnear, con-
fidently played by John Osborne, recognises the game that is being
played and covers his surprise and confusion. He acknowledges a worthy
opponent, and cracks a joke at the expense of his subordinates. Carter
shows him the respect due to a man who has achieved such a prominent
position in the northern underworld and who is, after all, an associate
of his bosses. He addresses him as 'Mr Kinnear', and accepts the more
familiar 'Jack' in return. But neither this superficial acknowledgement
of status, nor the apparently relaxed banter between the two men, can
disguise the underlying tension of the scene. Carter learns that his
brother worked in one of Kinnear's bars and, given the circumstances
of Frank's death, can hardly have missed the irony of Kinnear's instruction to good-time girl Glenda to dispense with 'those piddling little
glasses' for Jack's whisky and 'give him the bloody bottle'.

Adapted faithfully from the casino scene in Lewis's novel, the
sequence is structurally complex. Four conversations happen simultaneously: an intense exchange between Carter and Kinnear, the more
functional discourse of the poker game, the barbed banter between
Carter and the card players, and the flirtatious talk between Carter and
Glenda. The technical complexities were further exacerbated by changes
in the brightness of light coming through the windows, and by John
Osborne's decision to keep his delivery at low volume, a trait of real-
life referent Ronnie Kray. Hodges considers it the most difficult scene
in the entire movie, and regrets that he did not rehearse it more
thoroughly.[21] Certainly, there is a lot for the audience to absorb on
initial viewing, including the introduction of two significant characters
and information about Kinnear's links with Carter's bosses. The scene
exemplifies what is both the challenge posed to first-time viewers of the
film, and the pleasure to be gained from repeat viewings: the realisation

that almost everything that occurs in *Get Carter* has plot or character significance may be appreciated only at the film's dénouement.

The sequence at Kinnear's house ends with another sarcastic exchange between Eric and Carter, who alludes mockingly to the chauffeur's (and possibly Kinnear's) homosexuality in the line 'So it's all girls together is it?' Eric's sexuality is confirmed just before his last meeting with Carter when he says goodbye to the young man with whom he has spent the night at Kinnear's party. As Carter leaves 'The Heights', ironically the mansion that houses the Lord of the Underworld, his descent into a hell of his own creation is already in motion. What is effectively the first act of *Get Carter* is over, with the mystery established and the audience offered an apparently conventional identification with the protagonist. Carter, however, has yet to reveal all the facets of his personality.

A NIGHT IN NEWCASTLE

'This was the St James's Hall where boxing shows are held nightly. [...] The naked arc lights, the empty rows of seats, the awkward blood-stained fighters, the jeering spectators, all helped to make the scene an unpleasant one. I looked about me and thought I had never seen a crowd of men whose looks pleased me less. There was not one intelligent, sensitive face in sight. Or so it seemed in that harsh setting. [...] "Had enough?" asked my companion. I had.' J. B. Priestley on 'Newcastle life on a black wet November night', *English Journey*, pp. 293–4

Act two begins with a scene that is perhaps one of the few superfluous moments in the film. The brief interrogation of the scrap merchant near the King Edward VII railway bridge may be a way of establishing that there was nothing mechanically wrong with Frank's car, and provides Suschitzky with the opportunity to suggest the industrial dereliction of Tyneside, but it is questionable whether these considerations justify the lapse of continuity the scene represents. Carter has left 'The Heights' in the evening, but arrives at the scrapyard in daylight. If a day has passed, it has been one of very little incident and one unrecognised in Lewis's novel.

Continuity is re-established in the next scene in the Half Moon, where Carter refreshes his acquaintanceship with Keith the barman and learns that a man called Thorpe is asking questions. Hodges is rarely satisfied with simply the functional advancement of the plot, however, and this scene is no exception. Here, it supports the first of the film's explorations of Newcastle nightlife. As part of his careful research for the film,

Hodges had visited working men's clubs in the city and had taken care to cast his extras from among their performers and clientele. Again, Suschitzky uses fast film and a long lens to pick out Caine in the midst of the crowd, and record his amused reaction when a club singer's flirting with a man in the audience provokes an attack from his outraged partner. The two women involved, Denea Wilde and Tracey Star, knew and disliked each other, and, as with the confrontation between Caine and Hendry at the racecourse, their antagonism needed no further motivating. As the two combatants are dragged apart in a welter of spilt beer and exposed knickers, Carter makes his way back to the Las Vegas guesthouse, spotting Doreen in a snack bar on the way.

Doreen is with a friend and dressed for a night on the town, and she is less than keen on Carter's offer to take her away from the bright lights of Newcastle to some non-extraditable destination in South America. She is more delighted with the stack of notes she is given as a parting gift from her errant uncle/father. Carter's ironic encouragement in the shooting script to 'buy yourself some clean knickers', was dropped in favour of 'Be good. And don't trust boys.'[22] The location used was Bower's Cafe in Pink Lane, close to the railway station and the production team's HQ. The lane was notorious at the time for prostitution, and had once contained the offices of the dubious fabric business run by Dennis Stafford after one of his prison escapes in the 1950s.[23] The owner of the cafe, Ron Bower, was paid £50 for the four hours of filming that took place outside his establishment.[24]

PHONE SEX: LONDON/LAS VEGAS

' ... honest women are so seld and rare.'

Vindice in Thomas Middleton or Cyril Tourneur,
The Revenger's Tragedy, IV.iv.60

On returning to the boarding house, Carter picks up another *memento mori*, the ashes of his brother in a wooden casket that recalls the coffin from earlier scenes. The casket has much the same function as the ghost or the skull in Jacobean tragedy: it acts as a reminder of the revenger's motivation and a spur to the execution of revenge. The reception of the casket forms a macabre introduction to a scene that becomes increasingly bizarre.

The phone 'conversation' between Carter and Gerald Fletcher's wife, Anna, was filmed at locations 300 miles and many days apart. Apart from

7. 'Call girls are my business': Britt Ekland makes her contribution to a 'man's epic'.

posing for publicity photographs and filming the pre-credits sequence together, Caine and Ekland barely met. Certainly, Ekland's end of the conversation was filmed during the first day's shooting in London, and the uninhibited nature of her performance came as a pleasant surprise to her director: 'How far Britt went was totally her own business. Frankly, I was curious to see what she would give me, and she gave me more than I had anticipated. I was grateful because it made the scene.'[25]

Britt Ekland is now able to host television retrospectives of the 1970s on the strength of her performance, but at the time, she was filled with 'consternation' at being obliged to accept a part that she 'would not have contemplated under normal circumstances'. The collapse of her investment portfolio meant that she needed the £2,000 that Klinger offered her for a day's filming:

> For the first time in my life I came to realize the fate of less fortunate actresses who in order to earn sufficient money to survive on are forced to accept roles where they are required to strip off. [...] I had never done that before but Klinger to his credit respected all my wishes when I reluctantly accepted the role. The set was closed, the crew respectful and the director Mike Hodges was superb. I was not made to feel in the

least conscious about the scene in which I was seen lying partially naked in bed [...] Klinger was so delighted with my performance that he sent me champagne and roses.[26]

As Ekland peeled off her black underwear, apparently in response to Caine's instructions, Caine's part in the scene had yet to be shot. It was eventually committed to film at the Coburg Street location, with Rosemarie Dunham rocking noisily in the foreground as Caine spoke into the telephone mouthpiece. Between them rise a red candle and a glowing phallic table lamp. The resulting sequence, effectively matched and cross cut by Trumper, moves dangerously close to parody. That it manages to amuse and yet still retain an erotic charge is a tribute to the skill of the actors and Hodges' inspired decision to have Carter's landlady openly eavesdrop on the phone sex. The director admits that the scene was 'pretty crude' in many ways, but points to the importance of sound design in taking the edge off 'that slightly salacious side of it' and giving it 'a kind of lightness'.[27] Hodges and sound engineer Jim Atkinson use the sound of the rocking chair (augmented with a small bell) to build the scene to a climax, suggest Edna's growing arousal, and express Carter's sexual power. In a typically droll touch, one of Bob Penn's publicity stills taken on set shows Ekland stretched out on the bed with telephone in hand and a copy of *Man's Epic* magazine beside her. The lead story is 'Call girls are my business'.

The scene has proved to be the most controversial in the film as far as censorship is concerned. Hodges was outraged when ITV trimmed it in the early television screenings, and it was entirely removed by the South African censor, leaving cinema-goers wondering why Britt Ekland's name appeared on the poster at all.

THE DANCE HALL

'Down the front, mixing as quickly as possible with the current of the crowd, glancing to right and left of him and over each shoulder in turn. He could see no familiar face anywhere, but he felt no relief. He thought he could lose himself safely in a crowd, but now the people he was among seemed like a thick forest in which a native could arrange a poisoned ambush.' Graham Greene, *Brighton Rock* (1938) p. 8

The erotically charged atmosphere that has developed in the Las Vegas boarding house is finally broken by the arrival of Keith the barman, followed by a black sedan with Thorpe and three heavies. As the car draws up, the nervous and bespectacled Thorpe (a past acquaintance of Carter's) is contained by two frames within the frame: the vertical rectangle made by the boarding-house hallway, and the squarer frame of the car window. His insecurity is subliminally suggested, and confirmed later when he takes refuge in a toilet cubicle.

When Carter contemptuously dismisses Thorpe's gift of a free ticket back to London, the tension Hodges has so carefully built up over the first forty minutes of the film erupts into violence. Typically, it is sudden, shocking and short. The bloodied face of one of Thorpe's henchmen dramatically shatters the car window, and the car takes off, dragging a second henchman along by a stray seatbelt. As Thorpe goes on the run and seeks sanctuary in the Oxford Galleries dance hall, we are very much back in the *Brighton Rock* world of seedy lodging houses, sordid violence, a running man and a cheap *palais de dance*. The glowing marquee of the Oxford Galleries announces 'Big Beat Night' in blissful ignorance of the violence taking place in its environs. Inside, Thorpe in his flat cap and bow tie looks like a renegade from the 1940s among the floral mini-dresses and sharp suits gyrating to 'The Sound of the Seventies'. Carter seems unfazed by any environment, but as he stalks his quarry up the blood-red staircase and emerges on the balcony, we are once again given a hint that he is living on borrowed time. Hodges frames him in the circular scroll of an ornamental banister – an intimation of the telescopic sight in which he will be fixed at the moment of his death. The sign above his head reads 'Exit'. For the time being, however, he has an aura of invincibility. As he searches the toilets for Thorpe, other men avert their gazes and, when he finally flushes Thorpe out, a high-angle shot shows Bernard Hepton cowering in terror as if some avenging angel were about to descend from above.

In filming the dance-hall sequence Caine was given an insight into just how violent Newcastle nightlife could be when one of the formidable bouncers at the Oxford Galleries compared a typical Saturday night to 'Vietnam'.[28] That *Get Carter* drew on a world of clubland violence that exceeded anything in the movie was confirmed by Mickey Gallagher, a Tynesider who contributed to the film's soundtrack. Gallagher recalled the area's gang-controlled club scene for an article in *Later* magazine: 'You had your usual Saturday night scraps, but the vendettas were entirely different. You heard about them weeks before. I remember there were a couple of brothers at the Club-a-Go-Go. One of them chopped the head off an Alsatian dog. It was set on him, so he took an axe to it.'[29]

Hodges has confirmed a contemporary local newspaper report that a further sequence involving a fight in which a youth is thrown from the Oxford's balcony was filmed but deleted from the final edit.[30] Dramaturgically, the dance-hall brawl made more sense when it could be cross cut with the ballroom dancing competition originally scripted for the Oxford Galleries sequence.[31] Additional footage for the dance-hall scene was shot at Newcastle Airport's toilets because cramped conditions in the Oxford Galleries made camera movements difficult.[32]

'JOIN THE TEA SET'

' ... Do you put me off
With all your wild horse-tricks? Sirrah, you do lie,
Oh, thou'rt a foul black cloud, and thou dost threat
A violent storm!

Monticelso in John Webster, *The White Devil*,
IV.iii.100–03

With Thorpe secured for interrogation, Carter has to run the gauntlet of outraged working-class respectability from both his landlady and her priggish neighbour. He dismisses Edna's feisty attempts to exert authority by exploiting his sexual attraction for her and repositioning her as a spouse. She is condescendingly told to 'make a nice cup of tea'.

The scene that follows is remarkable for being one continuous take. Unconcerned that Caine spends much of the scene with his back to camera, Hodges abandons conventional cut-aways and shifts in camera position in favour of fluency. When he is not squeezing Thorpe's testicles or punching him in the stomach, Carter is handling objects which symbolise his brother's death: the casket containing Frank's ashes and the bottle of Scotch he extracts from his briefcase. Along with the whisky, Carter uncharacteristically swallows Thorpe's 'confession' that he is working for Cliff Brumby, a local slot machine distributor. Setting off to follow up this new lead, he adds insult to condescension by failing to drink the tea that Edna has brewed at his instruction.

As the darker aspects of Carter's personality are gradually revealed, our identification with the character may be becoming a tad uneasy. We may be asking the same type of question as the folksy embroidered plaque above the boarding-house bed: 'What would Jesus say?' The embroidery was discovered by Assheton Gorton (Hodges knows not where), but other than that, the interior of 25 Coburg Street was just as we see it in the film. Production design and set dressing were simply not required.

'THE PANTILES'

> ' ... because
> I am ignorant in whom my wrath should settle.
> I must think all men villains, and the next
> I meet (whoe'er he be) the murderer
> Of my most worthy brother.'
>
> Tomazo in Thomas Middleton and William Rowley,
> *The Changeling*, V.ii.4–8

One of the most common mistakes made in unravelling the twisted plot of *Get Carter* is that Thorpe is working for Brumby. This is a lie Carter is told to steer him away from his real persecutor, Kinnear. For example, Ali Catterall and Simon Wells miss the point when they assert that Cliff Brumby is one of those who want to 'get Carter' and that he 'sends his messenger "Thorpey" [...] to warn him off'.[33] On the contrary, Brumby quickly sees Carter as a possible confederate in his struggles with Kinnear. That Brumby knows nothing about Thorpe's activities becomes clear to Carter as soon as he sees the surprised and indignant reaction of the 'big man' to his intrusion (the antithesis of Kinnear's response to a similar situation). Caine registers Carter's realisation that he has been conned by the wiley Thorpe with a wry smile. 'I made a mistake,' he assures the irate Brumby, before having to warn him that, although he is 'a big man' he is 'in bad shape' and should therefore 'behave' himself. In Lewis's book, Brumby had been a distinguished-looking man 'in good shape', disadvantaged only by Carter's greater experience as a fighter ('Cliff, you're a big bloke, you're in good shape. But I know more than you.')[34] Hodges, however, was obliged to take account of Brian Mosely's rotund stomach.

The stomach is ideally suited to Brumby's character: a fat-cat businessman who personifies the bad taste of the upwardly mobile. Lewis's contempt for this class is evident in his observations of the clientele of Kinnear's casino, particularly the jealous and avaricious wives of the 'new Gentry'. Carter dismisses them as 'the kind of people who made me know I was right'.[35] When Lewis describes the moneyed sprawl of Scunthorpe's nouveau riche suburbs, he might be the sardonic Chandler describing the privileged enclaves of Bel-Air. The film perfectly captures the tone of Lewis's prose. Hodges had difficulty finding a suitable location for Brumby's home, but eventually settled on a house in Carville near Durham, and Assheton Gorton does a wonderful job in conveying the kitschness of Brumby's taste. Described in the script as 'a landscape gardener's nightmare', the garden is a riot of miniature windmills and ornamental fish ponds with ostentatious fountains. As Brumby returns from the police ball and parks his Rolls in the drive, he discovers a teenage *soirée* in full swing.[36] The raucous party, in what Hodges calls Brumby's 'prize possession', represents his tenuous hold on his social position.[37] He is over-reaching himself, and struggling to keep control of his businesses under the pressure imposed by Kinnear. When Carter walks though Brumby's continental porch with coach lamp decorations (in a shot that, with its depiction of activity through the house's windows, recalls Alfred Hitchcock's *Rear Window* [1954]), he is another intrusion in the big man's affairs. When he leaves, he has become a potential solution to his problems.

PURPLE UNDERWEAR AND PELAW HUSSARS

'Women are caught as you take tortoises.
She must be turned on her back.'

Flamineo in John Webster, *The White Devil*,
IV.ii.148–9

On returning to the boarding house, Carter discovers that Thorpe has been liberated, Keith abducted and Edna roughed up. Rather than showing concern and offering sympathy, Carter gets himself a glass of water so that he can take one of his pills. It is now clear to Edna, and to the audience, that he is a 'bastard'. She threatens to call the police, but Carter is confident of his sexual power. He knows the colour of her underwear and, like the alpha male heroes of romantic fiction, he rips her bodice to expose the purple symbol of her desire. But, for Carter, desire provides a means of securing co-operation. It is an emotion that can be manipulated if money fails.

In the sequence that follows, rather than being content with the classic narrative device of implying coitus by simply cutting from a seduction scene to the couple in bed together the next morning, Hodges introduces an inspired juxtaposition. Shots of the amorous couple are intercut with images of a girls' drum and kazoo band, the Pelaw Hussars, marching on the waste ground (now a school playground) opposite the boarding

8. *Bed and bawd. Carter and his amorous landlady (Rosemarie Dunham).*

house. For anyone who has seen Humphrey Jennings' seminal documentary about working-class leisure, *Spare Time* (1939), the marching band carries an unmistakable resonance. Hodges, however, seems to have been entirely unaware of the sequence in Jennings' film. Marching bands were a phenomenon he associated with the USA, and he was surprised to encounter them in the north of England. But if Hodges had not seen *Spare Time*, it would be very surprising if his cinematographer, with his background in the documentary movement, was also ignorant of the film.[38]

The shots of the Pelaw Hussars serve two functions. First, the innocence and optimism captured in the legend on their banner – 'For Youth and Valour' – offer a striking moral contrast to both the corruption of the city and the carnality of Jack and Edna as they sin under the plaque that asks 'What would Jesus say?' Second, they provide Suschitzky with the chance to show the physical contrasts of the city: the stand-off between the Victorian terraces and their replacements, the concrete and glass high-rise blocks. The no-man's-land between them is occupied by the Hussars, who are quickly joined by an equally incongruous red

Jaguar.[39] The car contains Peter the Dutchman and Con McCarty, the film's Rosencrantz and Guildenstern: two members of the Fletcher firm who have been dispatched from London to return their errant colleague to their employers. Carter trusts them as much as he would 'adders fanged', to use Hamlet's phrase.[40]

Peter and Con's invasion of Jack and Edna's morning intimacies is covered in a witty low-angle shot that reveals the shotgun and chamber pot beneath the shaking bedstead. The image virtually summarises the film's preoccupation with violence, sex and defecation. In *Get Carter*, 'shoot', 'shag' and 'shit' are as closely linked thematically as they are linguistically. Interrupted in his coitus, Carter has to move the pot to reach his shooter before standing up and pointing it at the intruders. That the phallic connotations of the long-barrelled shotgun are evident to all is made clear by the amused reactions of Peter and Con. Hodges milks the comedic possibilities by first filming Peter and Con through Carter's parted legs, a camera angle rarely seen outside of pornography (and perhaps hinting at a future plot development). The naked Carter, shotgun held erect, then follows the Fletchers' emissaries through the front door, causing Edna's nosy neighbour to spill her morning milk – an echo of Albert dropping his hotdog at the racetrack. There are enough visual double entendres to furnish a *Carry On* set, but Hodges' script keeps its eyes on the advancement of the plot, making space for Peter's barbed remark – 'If Anna could see you now' – which confirms his knowledge of Carter's clandestine affair.

With Peter and Con covering the house, front and back, Carter coolly dresses in his funeral suit and tie, handing Edna his briefcase and his brother's ashes in a deadpan parody of a domestic departure for work. Easily outwitting Con at the back gate, he shuts him in the privy and heads for his car, followed by Edna's plaintive appeal to him to return (she is clearly a glutton for punishment). Hodges was astounded, having seen Caine play a chauffeur in *Alfie*, to discover that his star had no driving licence, and had to ask Caine's regular stand-in, Johnny Morris, to take the wheel. Carter drives off down a back alley decorated with laundry hung between the crap houses, in a sequence that is one of the most imaginatively photographed and dynamically edited in the whole movie. Hodges and Suschitzky combine point-of-view, long, and low-angle shots in a rapid-fire montage as Carter roars into Coburg Street and rips the door off Peter's pride and joy. Con's frustrated cry of 'bollocks' as Carter speeds off was improvised by George Sewell and was still a shocking expletive for British films in 1971.

KEITH'S

'Some uncles are adulterous with their nieces,
Brothers with brothers' wives, O hour of incest!'

Vindice in Thomas Middleton or Cyril Tourneur,
The Revenger's Tragedy, I.iii.62–3

Carter's car, still festooned with washing, pulls up outside Keith's lodgings.[41] Jack's motivation is more than a purely altruistic concern for Keith's welfare. He wants to know the current whereabouts of Albert Swift. Keith lives in a poor, racially mixed neighbourhood where, judging by the inquisitive stares from windows, men in black suits are figures of suspicion. Carter is directed to Keith's room by an Asian housemate, and finds the badly beaten barman lying uncomfortably on his bed, the wallpaper behind his head covered in pin-ups and football memorabilia. As so often with the interiors in this film, the prominent colour of the *mise-en-scène* is brown, the colour of decay and defecation.

Keith has now also realised just what a 'bastard' Carter is, and rejects both his request for information and the cash he offers to 'square things'. The suggestion that the money will pay for 'a course in karate' provokes Keith into an outburst that rattles one of the skeletons in the Carter family cupboard: 'Frank said you were a shit, and he was bloody well right. You even screwed his wife, didn't you? The poor bastard didn't even know if the kid was his.' In the same breath that Jack is (once again) associated with defecation, the parentage of Doreen is questioned, and the bad blood between the Carter brothers is revealed.[42]

A VIEW FROM THE BRIDGE

'Heaven fashion'd us of nothing; and we strive
To bring ourselves to nothing.'

Antonio in John Webster, *The Duchess of Malfi*,
III.v.79–80

The scene in which Carter keeps his appointment with Margaret on one of Newcastle's principal landmarks, the Victorian High Level Bridge (the Iron Bridge), is crucial to establishing the film's sense of place. It is also central to *Get Carter*'s philosophical perspective of pessimism and its thematics of deception, rotten sexuality and moral contamination and decay. Like *Brighton Rock*, *Get Carter* is a depiction of man's incapacity

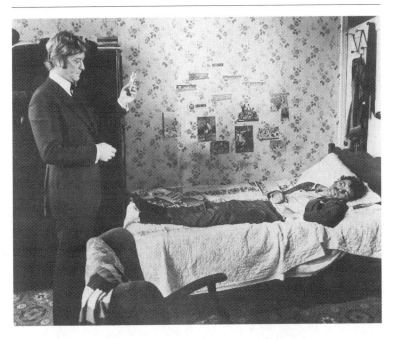

9. *'Get yourself a course in karate.' Carter pays off his helper (Alun Armstrong).*

to escape or transcend a fallen world. In the bridge scene, Carter and Margaret view the fallen city from a physically, if not morally, elevated vantage point. But their inability to maintain a lofty detachment from the underworld beneath them is confirmed by the arrival of Peter and Con's battered Jag and Carter's lightning descent to the quay below. When Hodges comments on the scene in his DVD commentary, he might be Graham Greene describing the environmental causes of Pinkie's social rise and spiritual fall in pre-war Brighton, 'the hell that lay about him in his infancy':

> The social content of this film is built into it. It's not a political statement but it's an integral part of the picture that, if you are brought up in these horrible situational circumstances like Jack was, you're not going to go back there once you're out of there, once you've escaped. [...] If he has to become a criminal, if he has to become a murderer, he will never, ever, be reduced to the circumstances of his childhood.

But, although Carter may have escaped his physical environment – the 'crap house' that is his home town – its cultural mark has been indelibly

10. *'We are what we are, like it or not.' Carter and Margaret (Dorothy White) on the High Level Bridge.*

inscribed by his socialisation. 'We are what we are, like it or not,' Margaret reminds him. If she cannot help being a 'whore', he will always be a 'bastard'. It is a vision of personal character as immutably fixed by social circumstance that the film seems to endorse. *Get Carter* does not share *Brighton Rock*'s faith in the possibilities of spiritual redemption. For the fallen, the moral high ground remains unobtainable.

Margaret continues to be defined by the excessiveness of her sexuality, here suggested by her attire: mini-skirt and sleeveless paisley top on a day Carter keeps his raincoat buttoned up. But the exposure of her flesh only heightens the secrets she conceals, once again symbolised by her dark glasses. When told a lie (that Frank had talked about suicide), Carter again removes a pair of sunglasses to see the eyes beneath, just as he had done with Eric. This time he snaps them and tosses them away to demonstrate his power and his contempt. He will break Margaret as he does her glasses, a fate foreshadowed in Margaret's irritated question, 'Why the bloody needle?', an unconsciously ironic reference to the fatal injection Carter will later administer.

With the arrival of Con and Peter, characters already associated with the waste matter of the body, Carter is again threatened with contamination when Con informs him that Peter is 'going to shit all over you'. It is Jack's cue to take to his heels and scramble down the bridge. In the chase that follows, Hodges and Suschitzky move rapidly up the gears, combining the scenic pictorialism of the earlier moments of the sequence with dizzying overhead and bumpy point-of-view shots, culminating in a striking high-angle view of the fugitive running across the quayside and finding protection in Glenda's white Sunbeam Alpine.

A FAIRY GODMOTHER AND A DEMON KING

'The office of justice is perverted quite
When one thief hangs another ... '

Bosola in John Webster, *The Duchess of Malfi*,
IV.ii.300–01

When Glenda, the self-styled 'fairy godmother', rescues Carter from his pursuers, and (self-reflexively) informs him that he is being driven to 'the Demon King's castle', *Get Carter* ironically acknowledges its debt to the folk tale of the hero's quest.[43] We assume that Carter is being taken to see Kinnear. Glenda was, after all, last seen on Kinnear's settee. Therefore, at the end of the hair-raising spiral ascent to the top of the Gateshead car park, it is a surprise to meet Brumby. Always ready to challenge convention, Hodges stages the meeting in a cavernous space that dwarfs the three figures. Brumby's voice echoes across an expanse of concrete, and Suschitzky again uses the favoured long lens to follow Carter's back as he slowly walks towards the 'big man'. By the time Carter is within a conventional conversational distance, the exchange is half over and we have learnt that Brumby is being forced 'to eat shit'

11. *The 'bastard' and his 'fairy godmother'. A post-coital Carter and Glenda.*

by Kinnear, who is keen to take over his slot machine empire. When Brumby names Kinnear as Frank's killer and offers £5,000 for his elimination, however, Carter reacts angrily at what he sees as blatant manipulation and an insult to his honour. He does not intend to be conned into targeting the wrong man again, and his vengeance needs no monetary incentive. He turns his back on Brumby and strides back across the expanse of concrete before being picked up again by the Sunbeam Alpine. It is unclear whether Glenda has been dispatched by Brumby as a 'sweetener' or if she is now acting as an independent agent. Lewis's book suggests the latter.

Although much of the dialogue in this sequence is lifted from the novel, the car park setting is entirely Hodges' invention. In Lewis's novel, Glenda drives Carter to the high-rise apartment that Brumby rents for her, in the time-honoured tradition of well-heeled adulterers. Hodges, however, is keen to make his setting carry a more contemporary meaning. The penthouse restaurant atop a multi-storey parking facility becomes an emblem of urban transformation and the rise of a new entrepreneurial class of barrow boys made good. Hodges describes Brumby as 'a new kind of Englishman coming up', and is sure that his rooftop eatery will be 'absolutely dire' because 'the man has no taste'.[44]

Despite their origins in different parts of the class structure, Hodges and Lewis share the perspective of an arriviste bohemian bourgeoisie, if not quite 'children of the revolution', then at least the vanguard of a new creativity. For them, men like Brumby are part of the flip side of the 1960s social revolution. These are working-class boys who no longer know their station, but who are neither educated nor geographically mobile. They have become the new bosses while rejecting all the protocols of civilised business practice and, in their wild ambition to be the new masters, they are recklessly transforming the cities of Britain. The Newcastle of *Get Carter* is Hodges' portrait of civic iconoclasm and Brumby's car park is its symbol: 'Everything is in transition. You get the sense of everything being pulled down and reconstructed, and it's got a temporary feeling about it. [...] It's a city on the cusp, a city that is going to be irredeemably changed.'[45]

TEACHER'S PET

'This strumpet serves her own ends, 'tis apparent now,
Devours the pleasure with a greedy appetite
And never minds my honour or my peace ... '

Beatrice in Thomas Middleton and William Rowley,
The Changeling, V.i.2–4

Finding original ways to shoot sex scenes is a perennial problem for directors. Hodges here finds a wickedly humorous solution, cutting between the journey in the high-revving Sunbeam and the anticipated coupling in Glenda's bed. The concept is beautifully realised by John Trumper, who uses the coverage of the suggestive movements of Glenda's hand on the gear stick, her pistoning legs on the pedals, the Sunbeam's frenetic rev-counter, and the amorous gyrations between Glenda's sheets, to construct a memorable sexual montage. The energy of arousal is wittily implied by the use of diegetic as well as non-diegetic sound, while the exhaustion after intercourse is represented by the switching off of the ignition and the empty exhaust pipe. With its extreme close-ups and visual innuendo, the sequence would not be out of place in a Russ Meyer movie, but Hodges does not let its camp humour overwhelm his narrative. His establishing shot of Glenda's grey high-rise block (now so redolent of the 'system-built' eyesores perpetrated by Poulson and his cronies) re-establishes a serious tone.[46]

It does not take much post-coital (verbal) probing from Carter for Glenda to realise, like Edna before her, that he is a 'bastard' who exploits sex to get information. Feeling used, she goes to run a cleansing bath. Carter is left alone to run the blue film in which Glenda stars and which Brumby likes to watch in bed. As the projector whirs into action, its buzz replacing the wheezing of the wind outside the tower block, we are reminded of the opening scene of the film. This time, however, laughter at unsophisticated northern sexual habits is replaced by tears. Carter experiences a moment of emotional epiphany as he sees Doreen being first procured by Margaret and then seduced by his erstwhile buddy, Albert Swift. The shots of Carter framed behind the reel of film evoke memories of *Peeping Tom* (Michael Powell, 1960), but Hodges and his production designer find a wonderfully effective solution to the technical problem of allowing us view the 8mm film and to see Carter's reaction at the same time. The projected image is reflected in the mirror behind the bed as the camera closes in on Caine's face as he registers the full horror of this slight to his family's honour. Caine's technique here is immaculate, conveying his character's shock with the subtle movement of the hand that holds his cigarette, a stiffening of the lips, and a glance away. As the spool unwinds its secrets, Caine's eyes glaze over and moisten, and as the reel runs out, so do Carter's tears. Usually the master of the gaze, Carter has now becomes its victim. We realise that his emotional armour can still be penetrated by sadness, but that the only way he can cope with sadness is to use it to generate anger and hate.

It appears that Michael Caine shared some of his character's distress. Never having seen a real porn film, he was apparently shocked that people would allow themselves to be filmed having sex.[47] It was a surprising sentiment for someone who, in this very scene, seems happy enough to nuzzle Geraldine Moffat's nipple.

Just as the ghost in revenger tragedy was substituted by Frank's ashes, the silent stag movie here replaces the 'dumb show' of Jacobean theatre and the Shakespearean 'play-within-a-play'. It supplies a concentrated visual revelation, a dramatic enactment of the justification for Carter's violent revenge. It is also an ironic reminder of the power of the medium itself. All the blood-letting, it turns out, is over a few minutes of soundless, monochrome celluloid, created to satisfy the appetite for voyeurism. It is, of course, the selfsame appetite we have indulged only moments earlier in watching Carter in bed with Glenda, and continue to indulge during the screening of *Teacher's Pet* as Hodges cuts away to a naked Glenda enjoying her bath. Once again, we are implicated in the same

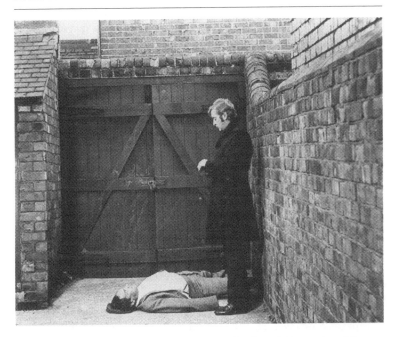

12. *A headache for the censor. The death of Albert (Glynn Edwards).*

guilty pleasure identified in *Peeping Tom*, and find ourselves included in the pathology of the gaze.

If the sequence in Glenda's bedroom implicates the audience in its critique of voyeurism, it is also highly self-referential. Producer Michael Klinger cut his professional teeth on 8mm 'glamour' films, and supplied Hodges with the reference material for *Teacher's Pet*. The film-within-a-film was the first footage to be shot on *Get Carter*, and was completed before the production unit went on location in Newcastle. Filming a porn pastiche at nine in the morning with a cast of strangers in his props man's home was a curious and uncomfortable introduction to feature film-making for Hodges. An awkward and unproductive first hour was finally turned around with the aid of cheap sherry, and an accurate simulation of a stag reel was achieved. Hodges recalls the whole experience as 'acutely embarrassing' and the films on which *Teacher's Pet* was based as 'about as erotic as a cold bath', but a rough cut of the scene in which Carter views the faux porn proved invaluable in convincing MGM executives that they had invested wisely.[48]

The moment Carter has completed his painful viewing of *Teacher's Pet*, and has turned his tears to anger, he turns his fury on Glenda. In an excitingly composed shot that breaks the frame into rectangular blocks as if it had been photographed by Mondrian, Carter ascends the stairs and brings a violent end to Glenda's peaceful ablutions. Having learnt that the film was produced by Kinnear, and that Eric was responsible for importuning Doreen, Carter begins his orgy of revenge with the luckless Glenda. Clearly blissfully unaware of Doreen's family connections, Glenda is nevertheless accused of deception and half drowned in her bath – an action which anticipates her watery end a few scenes later – before becoming a captive audience for Carter's assertion of family pride and a captive in the boot of her own car.

Hodges and Caine realised that the scenes in Glenda's duplex constituted the key turning point in the movie. Hodges has described Carter's reaction to viewing the stag reel as 'the nub of the film', because it reveals the complexity of Carter's makeup, the emotional life that is hidden beneath his blank surfaces.[49] The pressure created by the importance of the scenes, and the sudden emotional shifts within them, put Caine under considerable strain. By the time he came to do the bath scene, having filmed the others in sequence over the course of a day, he was decidedly keyed up. When the unfortunate focus puller ruined his first take, Caine exploded in anger. Unlike his character, however, he quickly showed remorse and apologised for his uncharacteristic outburst.

THE BETTING SHOP

'Let our hid flames break out, as fire, as lightning
To blast this villainous dukedom vexed with sin.'

Vindice in Thomas Middleton or Cyril Tourneur,
The Revenger's Tragedy, V.ii.3–4

The beginning of the 'third act' of *Get Carter* sees the revenger park the Sunbeam (with Glenda in its boot) on the dockside and take the Wallsend–Hebburn ferry in search of Albert Swift. From now on, the film gathers pace towards its bloody conclusion, and water – associated with purification and absolution – becomes a recurring motif. Close to the Hebburn ferry terminal, Carter bursts into a cafe in Ellison Street and begins roughly to interrogate a young mother about the whereabouts of Albert. Although the identity of the woman is revealed neither in the film nor in Hodges' screenplay, we assume that she is probably Albert's partner, because Carter recognises her and because she quickly telephones Eric when Carter leaves for one of Albert's regular haunts. As Carter strides purposefully down the terraced Argyle Street towards Ken Hailes' betting shop, where he expects to find his quarry, he passes walls covered in graffiti. One word stands out and fills a number of frames: 'FIRE'. It signals the ignition of Carter's deadly rampage.[50]

Discovering Albert in the bookie's, Carter asks him, 'Do you want to go to the toilet?' The phrase is a memorable one, not only because it extends the film's metaphorical concern with defecation, but because it cleverly references Albert's growing fear. Albert is clearly shitting himself and bolts for the back gate as soon as he is ushered into the bookie's back yard for his private business with Carter. By agreeing to accompany Carter outside, Albert is signing his own death warrant, but the look he is given allows for little opposition. Like a man before a firing squad, Albert is given a last cigarette before making a full confession. Eric's guilt is confirmed, and his link with Margaret is established, but Brumby's name is also added to Carter's hit list when he learns that Brumby's penchant for teenage girls, and his desire to find some point of leverage in his struggle with Kinnear, had led to Frank's discovery that his daughter was involved in Kinnear's blue movie business. It is a tangled skein of causality that is hard to unravel on first viewing, but the exposition provided in this scene is crucial to understanding Carter's subsequent selection of victims. Albert's pleas for his own life are in vain. According to the revenger's code of honour, Albert must die, not because he was responsible for Frank's murder, but because he has violated Doreen. His fate is signified by a shot over Carter's shoulder in which Albert's face is gradually obliterated as it sinks behind the black collar of his killer's raincoat. 'I know you didn't do it,' Carter reassures him as he plunges the knife home and watches the scarlet spread on his victim's white polo-neck. The killing caused concern to the censor, even though the two lunges of the knife are almost clinical in their execution and display, for the period, an uncommon restraint.[51] But, as Hodges has remarked, the impression of ferocity is amplified by the fury on Caine's face and his contradictory declaration of Albert's innocence. It is a fury born of 'self-hatred':

> A lot of Carter is self-hatred. You know he knows he's corrupt himself, so when he kills the people who have corrupted his niece/daughter, it's to do with himself as well and the knowledge that he really is sick as well. But in terms of the violence, if you look at the film carefully, it's actually on Carter's face and it reveals his own self-hatred and anger.[52]

A suggestion of Carter's ambivalent feelings was carried in Hodges' shooting script when Carter finally says to the dying Albert: 'Funny. You were my childhood hero.'[53] Hodges overdubs Albert's expiry with the mournful moan of the ferry's horn, as if to suggest the sound of the last breath leaving his body.

As Carter coolly returns through the betting shop, a blind punter (Tommy Early) in the foreground places a bet. Hodges had noticed the man when he had identified the bookie's as a suitable location, and used his sightlessness as a metaphor for the 'blind eye' turned to Carter's rampage.[54] The trope will be recognised by anyone familiar with *Brighton Rock*. Greene and Boulting place a blind man on the ghost train where Pinkie commits his first murder.[55]

The betting-shop sequence confirms that the earlier scene at the scrapyard does represent a lapse of continuity and that Hodges must be mistaken when he informs us in his screenplay that the action we have been following since the Pelaw Hussars' parade takes place on a Sunday.[56] Bookmakers do not open on a Sunday. This simple fact re-establishes Lewis's original calendar: Carter arrives on a Thursday for the funeral on the Friday, begins his killing spree on the Saturday afternoon, and meets his end on Sunday morning.

THE FERRY

'I have heard that Charon's boat serves to convey
All o'er the dismal lake, but brings none back again.'

Duchess in John Webster, *The Duchess of Malfi*,
III.v.105–06

Carter's return ferry journey is intercut with the arrival of a hostile reception committee, alerted by the phone call from the woman in the cafe, delivered by the mysterious Land Rover, and composed of Eric, Con and Peter. Working with the usual long lenses, Suschitzky films the ferry in documentary style, eventually dwelling on Carter's face as he gazes somewhat wistfully at some of his fellow passengers. Hodges' screenplay describes the look he gives to a mother with her two children as 'tinged with regret, even remorse'.[57] The regret is that 'he will never live that kind of life'.[58] Certainly, the lifestyle he has chosen renders conventional family life near impossible, but there is perhaps more to Carter's *tristesse*. As he looks at the children on the ferry, there is a sense of loss – not just of his brother, but of the innocence of his niece/ daughter. The family he has known has been broken and violated.

13. *Death is the ferryman. A German publicity still for* Jack rechnet ab.

The crossing of the Tyne assumes a symbolic significance . For Carter, a line has been crossed. He has finally moved beyond the restrictions of legality and conventional morality into a terminal world. Hodges is tempted to identify the River Tyne with the mythical waterway of the dead, the Styx, because his protagonist is 'moving all the time towards his death', but dismisses the idea as over-fanciful. He does, however, acknowledge that the river represents a boundary between one state and another.[59]

When the ferry docks at Wallsend, Peter (maddened beyond en-

14. *The big man's fall. Carter tips the 'Demon King' (Bryan Mosley) from his castle.*

durance by being made a fool of and having his car damaged by Carter) initiates a shoot-out, which results in his own death. Between the volleys from Peter's pump-action shotgun, Carter's adversaries take pleasure in telling him that they have informed Gerald Fletcher about his affair with Anna. Carter's face shows only a scintilla of emotion, but he knows now that all his bridges have been burnt. The future he has planned has also gone up in smoke, and his very survival depends on the destruction of all his enemies. Thus his crusade of vengeance has become a struggle for existence. The hunter is now also the hunted. For the moment, however, his surviving opponents beat a retreat, pausing only to deliver the mocking 'your car needs a wash' and shunting the Sunbeam into the Tyne. As the occupant of its boot drowns in terror, Carter's eyes register what might be a fleeting look of regret, before returning to their customary expression of resolve.

The formulation of this scene in the pre-production script is significantly different. First, the ferry is the car-carrying variety and Carter is driving Glenda's ailing sports car after his murder of Albert, when he is chased by Peter's Jaguar. Carter never reaches the ferry. Instead, with the full knowledge that Glenda is in the boot, he ditches the car from the end of the jetty, rolling clear just in time. Thus, he is directly responsible for Glenda's death, whereas in the filmed version he is simply powerless to prevent it. This change suggests a desire to increase audience sympathy for Carter, or at least to lessen antipathy. In the subsequent gun fight, Carter occupies the ferry waiting room while his adversaries take cover behind their car and a ferry worker's hut. Peter is unarmed when Carter 'cold-bloodedly' shoots him. The sequence was originally to accommodate four flash cuts of Frank's car going into the Tyne, Jack and Frank as young men out hunting, Jack and Anna making love on a beach, and Anna's face being slashed.[60]

If Hodges gave us time, the question might occur: 'Where are the police while all this mayhem is taking place?' Lewis tells us that they are paid to turn a blind eye to Kinnear's business, unless they are forced to act by complaints from the public. But with police co-operation vital to filming, Hodges avoids defaming the Newcastle force by avoiding the issue of corruption. In any case, Tyneside's bobbies do manage an appearance at the close of the sequence that follows.

BRUMBY'S FALL

'Pell mell! Confusion and black murder guides
The organs of my spirit. Shrink not heart:
Capienda rebus in malis praeceps via est.
[In evil dealings, the steepest way is the one to take.]
Piero in John Marston, *Antonio's Revenge*, III.i.222–4[61]

Retrieving the hire car that he parked on the quayside earlier in the day, Carter heads for Brumby's multi-storey. The 'big man' is still there, consulting with his architect and interior designer. Carter attacks him on the open car park stairs, confronting him with the consequences of attempting to use Carter's brother to put Kinnear in prison, before punching him into unconsciousness. In Lewis's novel, Brumby escapes with his life, but Hodges has such obvious contempt for the character that he allows Carter to finish the job. In a symbolic act of insurrection, he tips the 'Demon King' from his castle, his body crushing a car below and injuring its occupants.

The sequence is the most overtly political in the film. Despite his own profession, Carter seems to resent the exploitation of the weak by the powerful, represented here by Brumby's manipulation of Frank. By his inability to do his own dirty work, Brumby shows himself to be one of the contaminated, a 'shit'. But underlying Carter's disgust is a deeper hatred of social inequality. Just before he delivers the knock-out blow, he remembers witnessing the bacchanalia presided over by Brumby's daughter and venomously declares: 'Slags like your Sandra can get away with it, can't they? The Doreens of this world can't, can they?' Evidently, submerged beneath Carter's rank misogyny and violent individualism lie the vestiges of a radical conscience, as Hodges confirms: 'This is what Carter's about, to a large degree, anger at the predicament of poor people, deprived people.'[62] But Hodges' protagonist is unable to harness his cold rage to a political cause. Instead, his righteous anger results in 'collateral damage' to innocent bystanders, signalled by the warning alarm that sounds from the damaged vehicle beneath Brumby's body. For Michael Caine, the meaning of the injuries caused by Brumby's fall is that gangster violence cannot be ignored as something that does not affect ordinary social life. 'You're all involved in violence,' he assures listeners to his DVD commentary; 'it's not some separate world apart from you.' The political implications of all this, at a time when a Conservative government had just been returned, are subtly suggested as Carter roars out of the car park, passing under a sign that reads 'LEFT TURN ONLY'.

Hodges ends the sequence with a wicked tilt at the rapaciousness of those members of the creative professions who had climbed into bed with the nouveau riche. While Brumby's effete interior designer frets over his client's lack of manners and aesthetic sensibility, his more mercenary architect, spotting the arrival of the police, frets over their fees. In a film low on special effects, Brumby's ejection from the seventh floor of his car park stairwell is the most spectacular stunt. A lower part of the stairwell was used to film Caine tipping Mosley, an actor used to stunt work, over the parapet on to a hill of mattresses. A very realistic dummy was then filmed being thrown from an upper floor.[63] The 'collateral damage' was not in the shooting script.[64]

MAKING CONNECTIONS

> 'Make you to ravel all this matter out,
> That I essentially am not in madness,
> But mad in craft.'
>
> Hamlet in William Shakespeare, *Hamlet*, III.4.187–9

The two short scenes that follow Brumby's death show that Carter's rage has not subverted his cunning. Although he is mad enough to toss

Brumby from his car park, he is also crafty enough to plot the destruction of his more powerful enemies. In the sub-post office in Pelaw,[65] Carter mails a copy of *Teacher's Pet* to the Vice Squad at Scotland Yard as evidence against its makers. Perhaps with greater knowledge of the levels of corruption within Scotland Yard at the time, Lewis has Carter send the spool to a trusted journalist in London, and Hodges' earlier drafts of the script actually follow this lead. A large metropolitan firm involved in pornography like the Fletchers would almost certainly have paid dues to the Met's Obscene Publications Squad. For an appropriate fee, the spool would have most likely quietly have found its way back to its distributors. Carter's decision to 'grass' on Kinnear, however, does show his total estrangement from the underworld that has nurtured him. His abandonment of its codes is further demonstrated by his decision to involve a heroin dealer in his plot to snare Kinnear. As the women in the post office gossip about the news of the car park death, Carter phones to arrange a connection with the dealer on Newcastle's Swing Bridge.

Hodges films most of Carter's meeting with the dealer through the windows of the bridge's control box, cutting only to a direct close-up to establish that he is buying drugs and hypodermic needles. The mediated view recalls the celebrated scene in *The Ipcress File* in which Caine's fight on the steps of the Royal Albert Hall is shot through the glass panels of a telephone box.

MARGARET'S NUMBER COMES UP

'Hark, now every thing is still,
The screech-owl and the whistler shrill
Call upon our Dame, aloud
And bid her quietly don her shroud.'

Bosola in John Webster, *The Duchess of Malfi*,
IV.ii.175–8

Carter has purchased the heroin to kill Margaret and incriminate Kinnear. Tracking Margaret to the St James bingo hall (next to the Newcastle United football ground), Carter enters under a sign carefully framed to read: 'The Game is Final'. It is a further example of a trope which Hodges has used throughout the film to signal the imminence of death. And in another inspired use of 'found' sound, Hodges runs the bingo caller's response to a single shout of 'House' – 'checking just the one this time' – over a shot of Carter looking intently at Margaret. He keeps her under close surveillance when she leaves the hall, stalking her in the shadows like the Whitechapel Ripper, and finally confronting her in Salleyport Crescent with the chilling, 'I've come for you, Margaret.'

Hodges then throttles back on the building tension by cutting to Carter's phone call to Kinnear, blackmailing him with the threat of exposure to the police if he does not sacrifice Eric to Carter's need for revenge. The iconic image of Carter with the telephone receiver pressed to his ear is, unusually, used periodically during the film to emphasise his power and control, even at a distance. From the scene in the long bar, through the auto-erotic scene with Anna, to the call from the post office and this scene, Suschitzky's camera dwells on Caine's cobra-lidded eyes as he issues his instructions. Carter's call intrudes on one of Kinnear's parties in full swing, its unromantic couplings ironically mocked by the lyrics of Budd and Fishman's 'Love is a Four Letter Word'.

The phone call over, Hodges cranks up the tension again as Carter forces Margaret out of his car on the edge of Kinnear's estate. In a scene lit only by the harsh beam of the car headlights, Margaret is made to strip to her knickers before Carter, in a grim parody of sexual penetration, pins her down and injects her with a lethal dose of heroin. As an agent of bodily corruption, the drug is used as an appropriate punishment for the woman who has facilitated Doreen's violation. The headlights give the murder something of a *grand guignol* feel, but Hodges prefers to stress the role of the authentic light source in increasing the scene's verisimilitude. 'It is an unpleasant scene,' he has remarked. 'None of us liked shooting it […] It's such a lonely scene out there, and strange. He's circling round her like a tiger round its prey. It's a frightening scene.'[66]

FIXING KINNEAR

'And when they think their pleasure sweet and good
In the midst of all their joys they shall sigh blood.'

Vindice in Thomas Middleton or Cyril Tourneur,
The Revenger's Tragedy, V.ii.22–3

As *Get Carter* moves towards its brutal conclusion, its simple linear narrative begins to fracture and to develop parallel strands. Kinnear activates his final solution to the problem posed by Carter, using the co-ordinates supplied by Jack for his rendezvous with Eric. Unlike Carter's more hands-on approach to murder, Kinnear summons death as if it were a pizza delivery while watching live pornography (starring his party guests) on his close-circuit TV. Sex and death are frequent bed partners in this film, and the contract on Carter is no exception. The hitman, 'J', is sharing a bed with a woman when he receives his instructions to kill, and his victim's fate is sealed when he symbolically switches out the bedroom light.

Dawn breaks on Carter's last day with Hodges' camera panning across a classic English landscape to rest on Kinnear's stately manor house. Leaving the party, Eric bids his young beau farewell and climbs into his Cadillac (presumably Michael Klinger's car). It seems that the new aristocracy is no less debauched than the old. Suschitzky's long lens follows the Cadillac's progress until a sudden refocus reveals Carter's eyes reflected in his own driving mirror. Eric is already under his surveillance, and Hodges is once again emphasising the importance of the controlling gaze, and the eyes Eric and Margaret furtively hide and Carter uses to promote his power. Pre-eminently among actors, Caine appreciates how much can be conveyed with the eyes. As he remarks during his DVD commentary, quite often a scene is 'really about a look'. In the sequence that follows, we finally see the look of death as the camera focuses on the lifeless eyes of Margaret as she is dragged from the lake in Kinnear's grounds.[67]

With Eric on his last drive to the coast, Carter begins the film's endgame by summoning the police to raid Kinnear's party while he trails his prime target, Eric. When Carter parks his car at the towering coal jetty at Blyth Staithes, pockets his bottle of Scotch and cocks his long barrel, we begin the complex series of cross cuts – from the police investigation at 'The Heights' to Carter's pursuit of Eric – that Hodges has described as 'one of the best sequences I've ever been partially responsible for'.[68] The responsibility is only partial because substantial credit is given to John Trumper's rhythmic editing to Budd's echoing and increasingly percussive score. Suschitzky's beautifully detailed photographic compositions should also be added to the roll of honour. His camera gives Hodges and Trumper a full coverage of close and long shots and a wonderful array of angles that emphasise first curves, then diagonals and horizontals in a fluid geometry. We watch the line of police following the trail of clothing that leads to Margaret's body in the lake, we scan the line of party guests awaiting search and arrest, and we follow the jetty's rail lines as Carter chases Eric along them. The lines, like the destinies of *Get Carter*'s characters, are converging. Kinnear and Margaret are both being taken away, one in a police car and one in an ambulance. Carter and Eric are speeding across Cambois Beach to their final resting place on Blackhall Rocks.

GOODBYE ERIC

'I dare not look till the sun be in cloud.'

Vindice in Thomas Middleton or Cyril Tourneur,
The Revenger's Tragedy, IV.iv.118

For *Get Carter*'s final scenes, Hodges found the most desolate of locations. Blackhall Beach on the County Durham coastline near Peterlee is now the subject of a regeneration programme that will transform it into a nature reserve, but in 1970 it was a grim and unforgiving place, a terminal zone where the waste of the Durham coalfield was dumped into the broiling sea. When Hodges first gazed upon it on a freezing winter's day he saw its blackened sands shrouded in rolling mist and littered with the rusting remnants of abandoned vehicles. The vehicles, he surmised, had once belonged to seacoalers, people who had scavenged for fuel along the coast.[69] Their desperation had turned the sands into 'a sort of graveyard'. It seemed an 'absolute vision of hell'.[70] When Hodges returned to shoot the bleak closing moments of his film, however, he found the beach bathed in sunlight, destroying the atmosphere of despair he wished to evoke. Time is money in film-making, but Hodges resisted the pressure to begin shooting, waiting hours for the sun to go in so that Suschitzky could capture the blackness of the North Sea breakers and the dark silhouettes of the cable cars carrying their buckets of slag out to the ocean.

In this wild, untamed place, Carter is returned to a state of nature as a feral hunter. He chases Eric, who is in no better shape than Brumby, across the expanses of filthy sand before running him to ground just beneath the cable-car lines. He clearly intends to savour his climactic moment of revenge. Exhibiting that malign sense of humour that Eric so loves to mock, Carter stages a parody of his brother's death with the panting and gasping Eric this time cast as the victim. Eric is forced at gunpoint to guzzle the whisky (actually cold tea) until his ordeal is finally ended as the butt of Carter's shotgun crushes his skull. Fittingly, it is his victim Frank's weapon that takes Eric's life, just as it is (in slightly different circumstances) in Lewis's novel. At the end of *Jack's Return Home*, it is Eric who has the 'drop' on Carter, but the shotgun he is pointing in Jack's face backfires when the trigger is pulled, a twist Lewis may well have lifted from Mickey Spillane's *The Girl Hunters* (filmed by Roy Rowland in 1963). In a further parody of the cremation ceremony, Eric's body is loaded into a coal bucket and trundled away, like so much waste matter, to swell the slag heap out at sea. As a satisfied and joyful Carter watches, in deep focus, to the strains of Budd's baroque harpsichord, his shotgun resting jauntily on his shoulder, the body reaches the end of its journey and falls from its sooty bier into the waves.

The chase and killing of Eric was actually shot in reverse order because Hodges felt that a man as out of condition as Hendry might be in no fit state to play the death scene after running so far along the beach. It was a sad comment on the physical decline of a man who had captained his school rugby team and who, during his national service, had acted as a pace-maker for record-breaking runner Chris Chataway. Filming was jeopardised by the noisy activities of local teenagers, who were eventually pacified by liberal helpings of sweets and ice cream. The film company's largesse, however, did not stop the kids expressing their rebellious impulses by urinating on Eric's dummy before it was loaded into the dumper for its journey to the waves.[71]

DIAMOND CUTS DIAMOND

'Whether we fall by ambition, blood or lust,
Like diamonds we are cut with our own dust.'

Ferdinand in John Webster, *The Duchess of Malfi*,
V.v.71–2

On the face of it, Carter's death is sudden and unexpected. He looks at his shotgun, decides to dispose of it in the sea, and is shot through the temple in the act of throwing away his weapon. We do not see the sniper taking up position on the cliffs above his target, or the view through his telescopic lens, although we realise that in this final deadly gaze, he must have 'sighted' Carter. But rather than being a surprise, Carter's end has been prophesied from the very beginning of the film, and Hodges has constantly dropped reminders at intervals throughout.

The last intimation of Carter's death comes when we see the 'J' on the assassin's signet ring as he pulls the trigger of his rifle. The significance of the 'J' remains enigmatic. It may stand for 'Jack', suggesting the idea that Carter has been the author of his own death in taking on his crusade in the first place. Like a protagonist in Greek tragedy, the Aristotelian flaw in his makeup has finally proved fatal. Hubris has precipitated nemesis. The 'J' may further indicate that Jack has been killed by 'one of his own', a fellow hitman, one diamond-hard man to cut down another. Certainly, the professionalism of his killer is emphasised in the way he disassembles his rifle and wraps it carefully in cloth before quietly slipping away across the moors. Or the 'J' may stand for 'justice', the brutal reassertion of order that brings to a cold-blooded killer his just deserts; or even 'Jesus', the bearer of a divine justice that in the Jacobean cosmology asserts hegemony over the desires of man. In an only slightly more fanciful interpretation, Carter is a personification of man's evil, ritually sacrificed to cleanse the world of sin. He lies in a cruciform shape, the hole in his temple references the stigmata of a more noble martyrdom, and the water that laps around his head represents absolution. The eyes that burnt throughout the film with the cold fire of retribution are at last closed in peace. His resting place, as it so often is for the anti-heroes of gangster films, is in the purer environs of nature rather than the tainted zone of the city.

At the close of *The Revenger's Tragedy*, the protagonist Vindice declares "Tis time to die when we are ourselves our foes',[72] and at the end of his own killing spree Carter has demonstrated that he is no better than the men who murdered his brother. His evident pleasure in the torture and death of Eric places him beyond redemption, no longer an instrument of justice but a site of corruption. For Hodges, Carter's demise evinces the existence of a natural justice:

> There is a kind of justice. Even though it appears to be otherwise, we create the states we get ourselves into and, actually, that then dictates a large amount of the way we live and a large amount of the justice that may be meted out to us, if in fact we have not treated other people with respect and kindness.[73]

Whereas Michael Caine might secretly have 'loved him to walk away',[74] Hodges remains convinced that cold water needed to be poured on Carter's transgressive allure, and a moral closure imposed on a dangerously amoral story: 'I wanted him to be dealt with in exactly the same way he had dealt with other people. Now, that's a sort of Christian ethic in a way [...] That was a prerequisite of the film for me, that the hitman should just go [click] and that's it.'[75] But the theology of Hodges' 'Christian ethic' is far from simple, and is more Old Testament than New. 'Do unto others ... ' is a doctrine of perfection for a pious lifestyle, whereas Hodges' philosophy seems to be guided more by retributive ideas such as 'those that live by the sword ... ' and 'an eye for an eye'. The justice meted out on Carter is 'natural' only in a fallen society in which men murder their fellows for gain. After all, Carter dies at the hands, not of a *bona fide* representative of the law, but of a commercial killer (even though the irony is that, like Brumby's architects, he is unlikely to get his fee). The quasi-religious symbolism of Carter's death, then, may be impressive, but it is largely gestural.

In his book *Radical Tragedy*, Jonathan Dollimore warns us that the messages encrypted in the apparently conventional closures of Jacobean tragedy are not all they seem. Resolution of moral contradictions by recourse to the idea of 'poetic justice' is really only a 'perfunctory' closure, which merely papers over the cracks in the intellectual mortar of the text. What appears to be a formal restoration of political orthodoxy in fact creates space for oppositional readings.[76] Thus Jacobean drama sardonically inscribes a transgressive viewpoint beneath a conformist surface. Like its theatrical forebears, *Get Carter* is no straight didactic morality play, no simple struggle between good and evil. Carter is no avenging angel bringing divine retribution to sinners. He is not even Dirty Harry, the renegade cop who fights on the side of right. Carter is a hero who embodies, rather than transcends, the violence and rapaciousness of his world. His cause is egoistic rather than altruistic. If his death seems to take with it the ills of society, it is mere wish-fulfilment. Society, in all its grubby, graft-ridden glory, endures, and the future remains as bleak as a concrete car park.

THREE
Death and Resurrection

'Me mea sequentur fata.' [Let my destiny pursue me.] John Marston,
Preface to the first printing of *Antonio's Revenge* (1604)

Some New Years witness a quiet transition from one Christmas to the
next Easter, but 1971 was not one of those New Years. In Los Angeles
the trial of Charles Manson and his 'Family' was coming to its end. In
Uganda, a coup had installed Idi Amin as President. In Britain the year
began with the death of sixty-six football supporters when safety barriers
collapsed at Ibrox Stadium in Glasgow, and the bombing of the home
of the Secretary of State for Employment. By mid-February, the first
British soldier had been killed in Ulster, and maverick Tory Enoch
Powell had made his infamous 'rivers of blood' speech, calling for the
repatriation of immigrants. When *Get Carter* premièred in Newcastle
and London on 10 March, its 'fallen' and forsaken world hardly seemed
to exaggerate the violence and bitterness of its social context.

Get Carter's publicity campaign was starkly simple, centring on the
alliterative association of Caine with the role of Carter. The announce-
ments that 'Caine is Carter', and 'Carter is a Killer' accompanied an
image of a man with a shotgun on teaser posters for London transport.
The same conflation of star and genre dominated the film's British poster,
but in what seems a desperate and misguided attempt to suggest the
hipness of a genre that had largely fallen out of favour, Carter was
depicted in a pink tie and a floral jacket. Hardly the attire of a professional killer, this look had been out of fashion for a good two years by
the time of the film's release, and its use remains as unfathomable as the
reason behind Eric Paice carrying Carter's shotgun on the same poster.[1]
The American campaign ditched the floral jacket and emphasised the
film's identity as a violent underworld drama. Its posters carried an
image of a gun-toting Carter in the telescopic sights of a sniper's rifle,

15. *Killer in a floral jacket. The film's UK poster.*

and the question, 'What happens when a professional killer violates the code?' The agricultural long-barrelled gun was banished from publicity in favour of the more urbane pump-action shotgun. *Carter* was ready to confront the critics.

Initial critical vilification or indifference helps establish the conditions in which a cult can flourish. *Get Carter* had to make do with ambivalence. Graham Clark's review in the trade publication *Kinematograph Weekly* set the tone for *Get Carter*'s critical notices. Predicting a 'thumping great success' for a film with strong direction, script and performances, Clark qualified his praise with a distaste for 'a horrid story' of 'almost unrelieved, callous brutality'.[2] Few critics were prepared to go as far as the *Evening News*'s Felix Barker in unreservedly condemning the film as 'a revolting, bestial, horribly violent piece of cinema' made worse by being given a realistic setting, but many questioned the necessity for its scenes of graphic violence and its lacerating pessimism.[3]

Reviewers generally shared the opinion that the film's pleasures were guilty ones. George Melly, for example, confessed to shamelessly enjoying Carter's rampage, but likened the experience to 'a bottle of neat gin swallowed before breakfast' — intoxicating, but bad for you.[4] Although the *Daily Telegraph*'s Patrick Gibbs was condescending in his dismissal of the film's 'ridiculous' incidents and conventional characterisation,[5] his colleague on the *Sunday Telegraph*, Tom Hutchinson, was typical of a critical tendency to admire the power and professionalism of the film's construction while condemning its amorality and excessive violence.[6] Hutchinson likened Hodges' skills to those of 'a cosmetician at Forest Lawn', an appropriate simile for a director who had begun his film-making career with a documentary on the funeral business, but hoped that he would now turn 'to more worthwhile material'. John Russell Taylor in *The Times* disagreed, however, appreciating that the film's 'unpleasant' violence was integral to its effectiveness as a 'real' film:

> I suppose its unpleasantness will be held against it, but the tone is deliberate and I think something to be placed to the film's credit. Mr. Hodges may not have a very optimistic view of the way things are, but why shouldn't he? He does at least express his own gloomy view uncompromisingly and leave us to take it how we will. And he is clearly a talented film-maker.[7]

Other reviewers were prepared to overlook *Get Carter*'s violence in favour of celebrating its achievements as an effective thriller. Describing it as a 'tremendously exciting thriller', Ian Christie in the *Daily Express* told his readers: 'It is a cruel, vicious film, even allowing for its moments of humour, but completely compelling nevertheless.'[8] Richard Barkley in the *Sunday Express* and Fergus Cashin in the *Sun* both praised the film's acting and direction, while Ernest Betts in the *Sunday People* enthused that it was 'brilliantly made'.[9] Remarkably, no critics seemed to see *Get Carter* as offering a cogent criticism of the state of the nation or capturing a mood of the moment. If it epitomised any contemporary trend it was towards more uninhibited depictions of violence. Only the *Daily Mail*'s Cecil Wilson, in his evocation of *Hamlet*, related *Carter*'s tragic narrative of revenge to any tradition of European drama.[10] The film was viewed squarely as a genre piece, a tough-guy picture, for which the points of reference and comparison (positive or negative) were American. Thus, Dick Richards in the *Daily Mirror* was able to describe it as 'a gripping thriller that will take gangster fans back to the best of Bogart, Cagney and Edward G. Robinson'.[11]

In keeping with its perceived status as a genre movie, *Get Carter* was largely ignored at the BAFTAs, receiving only a single nomination – for Ian Hendry as best supporting actor. 'When *Get Carter* came out, it got slated for being too violent,' Caine recalled. 'Well, of course it's fucking violent. It's a film about violent people. We just wanted to make the violence realistic. To show gangster violence as it really was.'[12] Those who knew how it really was appreciated its realism: 'The real villains come out from the cinema and say it's one of the best pictures they've ever seen.'[13]

Villains may have enjoyed the film, but their support was not sufficient to put *Get Carter* among the top-grossing films of the year. In contrast to some of the mythology that surrounds the film, however, its box-office takings were very respectable. In the first week of its two-month London run, *Get Carter* broke the house record at ABC2, Shaftesbury Avenue (£8,188), and continued to do better business than *Up Pompeii*, which was showing in the larger ABC1. When moved to the ABC cinemas in the Edgware and Fulham Roads, it 'opened strongly',[14] in spite of strong competition from *Death in Venice* (Visconti, 1971), *When Eight Bells Toll* (Etienne Perier, 1971) and *The Music Lovers* (Ken Russell, 1971). On general release in the north of England in May, it enjoyed a 'very strong first week',[15] before falling victim to an unseasonal heatwave that decimated cinema attendance. In the south of England, the film had 'a highly satisfactory two-week run'.[16] Interestingly, although *Get Carter*'s downbeat and unsentimental tone is now thought to express the mood of its times, the mass cinema audience preferred *Love Story* (Arthur Hiller, 1970), which remained the most popular film in Britain throughout *Get Carter*'s run. Hodges is convinced that audiences found the graphic presentation of what he calls the 'Dickensian, Hogarthian [...] under-belly of my country' difficult to accept: 'I think the problem was that I was showing a side of Britain that people didn't want to see.'[17]

America was rather more used to hardboiled story-telling and, with a rave review in the influential trade magazine, *Variety*, the prospects for *Get Carter*'s simultaneous Stateside release looked encouraging.[18] The hip New York magazine, *The Village Voice*, hailed Michael Caine's 'best performance in years' and Hodges' 'unusual ability for combining the modern technical vocabulary – zooms, telephoto lens, self-conscious compositions, masking through natural objects – with a real feeling for the erotic and affective possibilities of a situation'. More prepared than British criticism to treat *Get Carter* as a serious work, it thought that the film was 'unabashedly aesthetical, flat formal, and implicitly socio-logical'.[19] The more conservative *Time*, however, recoiled at what it saw as 'a doggedly nasty piece of business made in blatant but inept imitation of *Point Blank*'. It acknowledged a 'first-rate, glacial performance' from Caine and 'brooding, striking photography' by Suschitzky, but felt the film's violence was 'a gruesome and almost pornographic visual obses-sion'. The result was that the movie 'wallows in its own ceaseless bloodbath and emerges like its protagonist – sleazy and second-rate'.[20] Given this level of heavyweight disapproval, it was not surprising that MGM allowed *Get Carter* to slip quietly on to the declining drive-in circuit as a support feature for *Dirty Dingus McGee* (Burt Kennedy, 1971).

Rather than putting money into promoting and distributing a foreign gangster film, MGM preferred to reinvest in a black-cast remake. *Sweet Sweetback's Baadasssss Song* (Melvin Van Peebles, 1970), *Cotton Comes to Harlem* (Ossie Davis, 1970) and *Shaft* (Gordon Parks, 1971) were demonstrating the potential of the films targeted at African American audiences, and MGM entered into partnership with Gene Corman[21] to adapt some of its properties as fashionable black action movies. Corman had already produced an adaptation of *The Asphalt Jungle* as *Cool Breeze* (Barry Pollack, 1972), when his reworking of *Get Carter* appeared in January 1973, just twenty-two months after the original.

In spite of its claims that it was an adaptation of Lewis's *Jack's Return Home*, George Armitage's directorial debut *Hit Man* was based directly on Hodges' film.[22] In Armitage's screenplay, Carter is renamed Tyrone Tackett, and South Central Los Angeles is substituted for Tyneside. Shot with long lenses in a naturalistic style that apes the earlier film, *Hit Man* also follows its narrative structure, adapting characters and locations to fit changed cultural circumstances. The understatement of *Carter* is replaced by a greater explicitness of representation. Margaret (rechristened Irvelle) is seen working in a brothel. Eric still wears his chauffeur's cap, but is now 'Shag' by name as well as by nature. Landlady Edna (now Laural), 'keeps her springs well oiled' and likes her man 'proud and erect'. Doreen (now Rochell) hands the money her uncle gives her straight to her boyfriend and, in one of the remake's rare plot departures, is killed by the porn mob. Its leader, 'Mighty Whitey' Zito, the 'honky faggot', is the film's principal white character. Brumby (now Theotis Oliver) runs sex shops rather than fruit machines, but is building a cinema for legitimate movie exhibition ('out of the porno, into the big time'). Glenda, or Gozelda as she is renamed, also has ambitions to move out of porno into a legitimate acting career. She is played by the woman who would shortly become a blaxploitation superstar, Pam Grier. The phallic Watts Towers stand in highly appropriately for the Tyne bridges, and an illegal dog fight makes a very acceptable substitute for Newcastle racecourse.

Hit Man's dialogue attempts to capture the authentic vernacular of black urban society, but it falls short of the terse poetry of *Get Carter*, and the delivery is sometimes slow and wooden. Armitage, however, is

highly astute in his cultural conversions. Situating his drama in Los
Angeles' used-car culture of 'repo men' and burgeoning porn marketplace, he manages to make timely observations on both the hidden
underbelly of Hollywood and the moral disintegration of African
American society. His most inspired conceit is to have his Albert Swift
character (Julius) moonlight as a porn stud while working at the 'Africa
USA' safari park at Fillmore. When Tackett (Bernie Casey) arrives there
to throw the fallen Gozelda to the lions, the idea of returning home is
given even greater resonance than in Hodges' and Lewis's texts. But,
in spite of its higher body count and greater explicitness, *Hit Man*
ultimately pulls its punch by having its protagonist survive the attentions
of a police assassin on Terminal Island. In its enthusiasm to present
Tackett as a noble lion (an 'Ebu chieftain') in a jungle of white-sponsored
moral corruption, the film forgets that, in his excessiveness, sexism and
profession as a gangster, he is far from being a racial exemplar.[23] At the
same time, it turns itself from poetic tragedy into a more prosaic action
thriller.

GONE BUT NOT FORGOTTEN

'Quite often, you only realize how good a film is in retrospect. It'll come
out, do a bit of business. Then years later, a whole new generation picks
it up and hails it as a classic.' Michael Caine, *Loaded*, 58, February 1999

As a British genre film released at a time when such texts were rarely
deemed worthy of sustained analysis, *Get Carter* received little attention
in the literature of film studies. True, in the year following its release,
Thomas Elsaesser selected it for criticism in his appraisal of the state of
British cinema in *Monogram*, but only to illustrate the poverty of a
national cinema too much in thrall to Hollywood:

What might have been a sombre accumulation of *actes gratuits* to give
an image of unrelieved evil and degradation shrinks from its own nihilism by having a stock revenge motif plugging all the gaps – which is
furthermore grafted on a sentimentality difficult to bear (Michael Caine
sobbing as he watches his niece being seduced in a blue movie) let alone
take seriously.[24]

Elsaesser, then, has the distinction of being perhaps the only com-
mentator to find Hodges' 'protracted sado-masochistic fantasy' both too
conventionally motivated and too sentimental, but then most ignored it.

Although the critic Alexander Walker ironically placed the image of Carter with his pump-action shotgun on the cover of his book on 1970s British cinema, *National Heroes*, most preferred not to mourn for the film.[25] *Get Carter* was simply not the kind of text that the fledgling discipline of film studies wanted to discuss. Any notoriety it may have acquired as a cinematic *bête noire* was quickly obliterated by the wave of controversy that accompanied the release of *The Devils*, *Straw Dogs* and *A Clockwork Orange*, all within a year. If there was any examining of contemporary film-making in Britain to be done, these disturbingly violent films from acknowledged auteurs were first in line for consideration. Consequently, *Get Carter* spent twenty years in the critical wilderness. When, on a rare occasion, a cineaste was obliged to remember the film, it was to lament the passing of a once virile film industry now withered by lack of American finance. In the darkest days of British cinema, Derek Owen wrote an entry on Mike Hodges for *Film Dope*. He argued that Hodges' career was indicative of the squandering of talent that accompanied the collapse of indigenous film-making in the 1970s, noting that the director had made 'one of the most accomplished debut features since the war' and describing *Get Carter* as 'worthy of Siegel at his best'.[26]

The film remained virtually absent from critical discourse in the decade following Owen's comments. *Get Carter*'s nihilism and unsentimental portrait of the working-class community made it few friends among left-liberal critics. Its comments on the climate of corruption in northern cities – so prescient in the light of the Poulson/T. Dan Smith scandal that quickly followed its release – went largely unacknowledged. The unorthodoxy of its ideological position left the film exposed in the prevailing climate of political correctness of the 1980s. Its emotional hardness and the blatant misogyny of its protagonist made it difficult to champion as the strength of feminist criticism grew. In a film culture largely dedicated either to sniping at contemporary political policy or evoking the visual splendours of the past, a vigilante movie in which a unreconstructed male seeks personal revenge in a half-reconstructed city was always likely to be marginalised. Where was the 'new man' with his more flexible and progressive construction of masculinity? Where was the new city with its vibrant multi-ethnicity and aesthetic regeneration (its beautiful laundrettes)? It does not take long for a state-of-the-nation film to become a dinosaur. Rarely seen on television and unavailable on video, Hodges' tale of predators in the urban jungle was turned into a ruminant and put out to pasture.

The keepers of *Get Carter*'s flame were a motley and unfashionable bunch. The faithful in the north passed on the oral tradition of the film in pub badinage ('Do you want to go to the toilet, Albert?'), and some semblance of a public presence was maintained within the music business by first the Human League, who covered Roy Budd's theme music on their best-selling album, *Dare* (1981), and then in the name adopted by die-hard punk band Carter the Unstoppable Sex Machine. In his book on heritage and the national past, *On Living in an Old Country*, Patrick Wright refers to England in the early 1980s as 'a country which was full of precious and imperilled traces – a closely held iconography of what it is to be English – all of them appealing in one covertly projective way or another to the historical and sacrosanct identity of the nation'.[27] The memories of *Get Carter* were among those 'precious and imperilled traces'. For its fans, the iconography of the film encoded powerful truths about a fast-disappearing social, industrial and gender order, truths vulnerable to the sanitising and prettifying imperatives of the merchants of heritage. The rough, tough and unforgiving Tyneside recorded in the film's photography and ethnography acquired the status of 'the world we have lost', a more authentic locale than the design-conscious, mediated, feminised environments promoted by Thatcherism. Caine's knight-without-honour carried the memory of an unchallenged patriarchy, a time before the 'iron lady' when action was a male preserve, and 'power dressing' meant putting on a black trenchcoat.

Bruce Kaywin has argued that cult films have a 'personality' that matches some quality in ourselves as viewers, however dark, repressed and other.[28] The viewing experience brings with it the frisson of recognition. For those who turned *Get Carter* into a cult, then, the film carried the essences of the past, honest and unrefined in their depiction of dishonesty and lack of refinement. The film, and the memories of its enduring audience, constituted part of what Wright calls that 'vernacular and informal sense of history' that resists the mythologising of the past by architects of national identity.[29] Michael Brady, the author of a Web site dedicated to identifying all of the locations used in *Get Carter*, describes the film as 'a time capsule'. Born in the year *Get Carter* was filmed, two streets away from the terrace in Benwell where Frank Carter's house was situated, Brady has no recollection of the streets (now demolished) where he spent the first two years of his life. The film fills in the gaps in his memory, effectively reconstructing the geographical ambience of his childhood: 'I suppose it's this local touch which makes the film so special in my eyes.' The streets that he had forgotten are depicted in this period piece 'for all the world to see, with a star-studded cast'.[30] For Geordie fans like Brady, the film negotiates the gulf between the public and the private, the present and the past.

A similar relationship with the past informed the eventual formation of the *Get Carter* Appreciation Society in 1999. Surprisingly, the society was an offshoot from the larger *The Prisoner* Appreciation Society,[31] and is composed of a small group of middle-aged enthusiasts of both sexes. As local researcher Amy Redpath discovered, members come from a wide variety of backgrounds, with occupations ranging from university porter through librarian and veterinary nurse to solicitor.[32] The group meets regularly in the Bridge Hotel public house on the banks of the Tyne, where the devotees of the film can gaze at Newcastle's Iron Bridge, the location for what the group agrees is one of the most magnificent scenes in film history. For local fans, the setting is as important as the film's action in determining its significance: 'The magnificent Tyne Bridge, the river rippling below. Michael Caine poised against the backdrop of the remnants of the North East's industrial metropolis. The claustrophobic atmosphere of the bridges all around ...' The film is seen as validating pride in regional identity and an unsentimental interest in the changing local landscape and industrial infrastructure, but its status as a document that carries its precious historical images to a national and international audience is equally important. As the society's convener, Chris Riley, puts it, '*Get Carter* is an archive of the north east in the 1960s, and this legacy needs to be preserved for future generations.' As a social document, the film is of particular importance because 'instead of taking a top-down approach to north-eastern life, it takes a bottom-up one'.[33] It is thus significant in class as well as geographical terms. The tragedy of *Get Carter* stands in for and represents the tragedy of the north east, a region crippled by the decline of heavy industry and the erosion of its manufacturing and coalmining base, and blighted by the irresponsible brutalism of its town planners. The film must be promoted if only to show the death that preceded the rebirth of the region in a post-industrial age. Thus, part of the motivation for the society's organisation of a tour of the film's locations is to change outsiders' perceptions of the area, to erase the image of 'a mass of slums, extreme deprivation and poverty', and to enhance the viewing experience of non-Geordies by creating a more intimate relationship with the locales depicted. For many of the hundred or so fans from the south who trekked to Newcastle for the society's tour in 2000, however, part of the appeal of the film resides in the exotic 'otherness' its locations evoke.

For them, *Get Carter*, with its Cockney star, may be the story of a London lad who leaves his natural environment to go north into a less sophisticated world, and almost succeeds in defeating impossible odds. Jack is not so much returning home as, to use an imperial analogy, going to deal with restless natives. In terms of cultural familiarity, they may feel that the film is nearer to *Zulu* than to *Alfie*. Remarkably, *Get Carter* seems to work equally well for both Tyneside and Thameside audiences as an emblem of local masculine pride.

It is significant, however, that the organisation of fan activity for *Get Carter* post-dates the film's availability for home viewing. Without video release, the cult of Carter had limited access to its sacred text and no means of recruiting new members. *Carter* was screened in a bowdlerised version by London Weekend Television in 1976 and 1980 but, apart from a single broadcast by Westward Television, it remained unseen by viewers outside the London area until the BBC picked it up in 1986 and screened a late-night, uncensored version. In 1993, however, MGM/UA quietly issued *Get Carter* as part of its 'Elite Collection' range of videos distributed in the UK by Warner Home Video. There was no advertising to suggest that a significant event had occurred. It was simply a part of the long process of exploiting MGM's back catalogue in the run-up to Christmas. Reviews were sparse, but a hint of things to come was evident in the full five stars and small illustration that accompanied *Empire*'s assessment of the film as 'one of the best British films of the 70s'. It did not find a place, however, among *Empire*'s top fifty videos of the year.[34]

Although it went largely unheralded at the time, the release of *Get Carter* on sell-through video was important in developing its popularity. As Robert Murphy has pointed out, the convolutions of *Get Carter*'s plot are more easily unravelled with the opportunities of rewind and repeated viewing that video provides.[35] Enthusiasts could also disassemble the text, going over favourite (but frequently misquoted) snatches of dialogue, and engaging in the textual 'poaching' so significant in the creation of a cult film.[36]

The availability of the film was a necessary, but hardly a sufficient, condition for its successful revival. What was needed was a change of critical climate and an association with cutting-edge contemporary film-making. Both were supplied by Quentin Tarantino.

One crucial side-effect of the media feeding frenzy that followed the production of *Pulp Fiction* (1994), Tarantino's follow-up to *Reservoir Dogs* (1992), was the creation of new regard for the wellsprings of his cinema. The immediate beneficiaries were the blaxploitation films of the

1970s and the reputations of hardboiled writers like Jim Thompson, David Goodis and Elmore Leonard, but the 'Tarantino effect' also had its impact on British cinema. Danny Boyle and a brat pack of would-be hipster directors tapped into the knowing, cynical, cine-literate sensibility important to the appreciation of Tarantino's amoral entertainments, but a casual remark by the *wunderkind* brought *Get Carter* back into fashionable consideration. Tarantino had seen Hodges' film at the Nuart Theatre in Santa Monica on a double bill with Robert Altman's *The Long Goodbye* (1973) and been so impressed that he did not bother staying for the main feature.[37] At a crime film festival in Nottingham in 1993 he named *Carter* first among his favourite British films.[38] As if a high priest had pronounced a humble artefact sacred, *Get Carter* acquired an aura that confirmed the faith of the devoted.

CARTER GETS *LOADED*

' … are not my lines
Right in the swaggering humour of these times?'

John Marston, 'The Author in Praise of His Precedent
Poem' (*c.* 1598)[39]

Although it is difficult to overstate the influence of Tarantino, particularly for young male film fans, during this period, even the most charismatic individual needs a conducive cultural context and a receptive audience to become an arbiter of taste. There is evidence, in Britain at this time, of a significant attitudinal shift in the demographic group that made up Tarantino's core audience. The spring of 1994 saw the successful launch of an irreverent new magazine, founded in opposition to the prevailing orthodoxies of the male style press. *Loaded* was described by one of its editors as 'an anti-men's magazine' and it sought to tap into 'a certain English […] laddishness' that was 'in the air' in the early 1990s and with which the established young men's publications seemed 'laughably out of touch'.[40] Produced for men who had experienced a commercialisation and feminisation of society in the 1980s, *Loaded* offered a jocular and ironic discourse on masculinity and nationhood that posed in jaunty opposition to the doctrines of political correctness. Aesthetically, culturally and politically, *Loaded* was infused with nostalgia for a mythic 1970s when fashions were 'naff', culture was irony-free, gender politics were straightforward and definitions of the nation were narrow and exclusive.

What most commentators underestimated, however, was the degree

16. *A film for the lads? Carter is chatted up on his first meeting with Glenda.*

to which *Loaded*'s ironic celebration of post-feminist roguishness was embedded in a vernacular and class-conscious conception of Englishness that deplored the cultural exclusion of 'ordinary' and 'everyday' experience. When *Loaded* journalist Jon Wilde came to articulate the magazine's dissatisfaction with the cant that passed as a public definition of national identity, there was a clear echo of Mike Hodges' denunciation of the cultural hypocrisy and myopia that motivated *Get Carter*:

> I got this sudden realization that *Loaded* had clocked on to the fact that there was another kind of Britain other than the Beefeater, fucking poncing around in Florence [*A Room with a View*], that kind of highbrow Britain. *Loaded* clocked on to what we all knew anyway; there was another England but no one had ever championed it. In fact people felt genuinely embarrassed about it.[41]

For the constituency of *Loaded* and the 'lads' mags' that followed its lead, *Get Carter* was a perfect example of that other England, an unjustly neglected repository of robust vernacular realism and masculine lore. If England and its national cinema had been softened by elitist aestheticism and bourgeois formulations of heritage, here was the ideal antidote: the tragic story of a hard man in a hard city, a memo from purgatory.

In November 1995, Martin Green and Patrick Whittaker included four extracts from the *Get Carter* score in their film soundtrack compilation *The Sound Spectrum*. *Loaded* needed no further excuse to feature a double-page photograph from the film and to recommend it as 'a 70s classic with a soundtrack to boot'.[42] *Get Carter* was serialised as a cartoon in *Loaded* in summer 1996 (June–September), and Jack Carter might have been the ideal character to deliver one of *Loaded*'s favourite ironic catchphrases: 'Come on then, if you think you're hard enough'. A decade earlier, when the pioneer men's style magazine *Arena* had featured an eight-page article on Michael Caine, liberally illustrated with images from his films, the only reference to *Get Carter* was in an accompanying filmography.[43] With the 1970s not yet back in vogue, it was Caine's portrayal of Harry Palmer, rather than of Jack Carter, that made him an icon of style. When *Loaded* published a very similar retrospective on Caine in 1999, however, *Carter* was featured prominently as the definitive Caine movie – 'What can you say? British pulp noir at its finest.' It was one of 'our most dearly beloved films of all time'.[44]

Where *Loaded* led, other young men's magazines were quick to follow. In the spring of 1997 the film monthly *Neon* named *Get Carter* as one of the '100 films you must see before you die'.[45] A few months later, MGM reissued the film on video as part of a series of twelve 'Modern Classics', and *Neon* used the occasion to run an interview with the director of what it described as 'the best crime thriller this country has ever produced'.[46] *Empire* selected the video as its recommended-to-buy release of the month, confident that the film was a 'landmark' in British cinema.[47] The specialist crime fiction magazine, *Crime Time*, made *Get Carter* its cover feature, boasting an exclusive article by Mike Hodges and a profile of Carter's creator, Ted Lewis. The magazine endorsed its interest by evoking a fashionable Tarantino connection: 'Tougher than *Reservoir Dogs* … cooler than *Pulp Fiction*'.[48]

Get Carter's 'coolness' was further promoted by the commercially successful release of its soundtrack at a time of unprecedented interest in film music, and the film's path to acceptance by a young audience was smoothed by the growing vogue for its period, the 1970s. The decade began to be valued not only as a source for retro fashions, but as a moment of unselfconscious hedonism before the arrival of puritan political correctness. Although Ang Lee treated the permissiveness of the era with scepticism in *The Ice Storm* (1997), new *wunderkind* director

Paul Anderson was happy to celebrate 1970s pornographic film-making in *Boogie Nights* (1997). *Neon* featured his film on the cover of its '70s issue' of February 1998. *Carter*, of course, had taken a rather more critical look at the blue movie business, implicating it in murder and the corruption of innocence.

The indications given by the types of magazines that began to champion *Carter* in the 1990s are that it is predominantly men who like the film. No one would claim that those who register their votes in the Internet Movie Database (IMDB) poll are a representative sample of film-watchers, and a preponderance of male respondents is a familiar feature of this type of interactive exercise on the Web, but the scores and demographic breakdowns for *Get Carter* are striking. By April 2002, two-thirds of 1,361 voters had awarded the film at least eight marks out of ten, giving a mean score of 7.9. Less than 6 per cent of these voters were women (53 of 947 declaring their sex). The average score awarded by male voters was 11 per cent higher than that of female voters. If we compare these figures with those of eighteen months earlier (October 2000), the only really significant change is in the number of people registering their vote. The increase is 300 per cent, astonishing for a thirty-year-old film, and a revealing measure of *Carter*'s new stature.[49] Awarding the 'landmark British film' a 'perfect 10', one male correspondent from Wales declares that he has 'watched the film so many times that I don't think I'll ever get bored of it', while another from Yorkshire asserts that it will always remain his 'number one film'. Another from Wolverhampton makes it clear that *Get Carter* is 'not only the best British film, but the greatest movie of all time'. The film is valued for its 'realism', 'honesty', believability, coldness, and grit – all of which are seen to be exemplified by its atmospheric settings, dark humour and bleak surprise ending. Equally important are Caine's impassive (minimalist) performance, and the character of Carter. Mark Benn of Brighton emphasises the importance of the way in which a more sensitive and vulnerable aspect to the personality of an apparently cold-hearted killer is gradually revealed in the course of the film. Darren Burns of Manchester is attracted to the irresistible force that Carter embodies: 'It always reminds me of The Terminator – a ruthless, unstoppable force that is not to be messed with.' Many fans are also able to relate to Carter's mood of cold fury and his quest for a justice the law is unable to provide.[50]

If *Get Carter* is able to encapsulate for its modern male admirers a raw, passionate and dangerous potency tragically lost, what does it represent to female viewers? Clearly, the film is easily readable as a depiction of patriarchal power within a dominant homosocial order. Moreover, its female characters are subject to Carter's traditional bipolar classification of women as Madonna or whore (a name he calls both Margaret and Glenda), those who wear purple underwear and those who don't. Whores are expendable and deserving of punishment, while Madonnas like Doreen require their virtue to be defended to the death. Of the whores, two die, one is disfigured (offscreen) and one is the victim of rough treatment. There is no question that the film's protagonist has internalised a sexist belief system, but does the film itself endorse his views? The director's response to criticism of his film's treatment of women is not entirely reassuring. First Hodges asserts that at least women are not peripheral in *Get Carter*, but occupy significant roles in the narrative. Second, he argues that Carter's protective sentimentality towards Doreen mitigates his casually misogynistic treatment of other women. Third, he points out that Carter regards everyone (not simply whores) as expendable.[51] None of these arguments really challenges Carter's sexism. It is hardly surprising that one of the few women to review the re-release of the film, Antonia Quirke, remained unconvinced about its ability to condemn the world-view of its central character. For Quirke, the hero of the film is representative of those men 'who have no desire to uncover the paradoxes within themselves [...] men who kill as though it were the perfect one-night stand'.[52] But, like George Melly and his morning gin, she realises that such men can be bad but intoxicating: 'Carter smells of a psychopath, and we love a nutter. But only when they're men.'[53] Her unease with the sexual politics of the film recalled that of Nina Hibbin in her review of *Carter*'s original release: 'With confidence, cynicism and considerable skill [Hodges] plays upon all those complex and suspect elements which go to make up the English tough guy image. He has made a film that is rather sick.'[54] Hibbin implied that Hodges – a director she believed to have 'the potential for an altogether different kind of film-making' – had knowingly manipulated the signifiers of rugged masculinity to maximise the box-office potential of his film. Evidently, neither woman felt that the frequent adverse judgements passed on Carter by his female victims, the calculated exposure of his sexual double standards, and his ultimate punishment at the film's closure, were sufficient to negate the appeal of his predatory sexuality.[55]

When Amy Redpath asked one of the female members of the *Get Carter* Appreciation Society, a thirty-one-year-old veterinary nurse, about the film's appeal, she received a more solidly post-feminist and post-modernist response. Sexual attitudes appeared to be less significant than

17. *'Whores are expendable': Carter disposes of Glenda in a shockingly misogynistic fashion.*

Carter's locations and period details like cars and clothes. Attitudes were to be taken as representative of their time, and in contradiction to most feminist theories of representations, Carter was to be viewed as 'just a character in a film and nothing more'. The character of Carter, however, in spite of his brutal treatment of women, was undeniably appealing. Far from acting as a repellant, his image as a 'bloke's bloke' and a 'bad boy' presented a challenge: 'I like the fact that he is dangerous, but I bet I could tame him!' Carter, she felt, needed to be tough if he was to see through his righteous mission of revenge. His death was to be regretted: 'I always think that it's a real shame that he gets shot at the end of the film after he has avenged his brother's death and everything; it seems such a waste.' This female fan remained surprised that more women did not find pleasure in *Get Carter*, a lack she attributed to the offputting label of 'gangster film'.[56] The IMDB does offer some evidence of a growing engagement with the film on the part of women. In the eighteen months before April 2002 the rate of increase in women voting on *Get Carter* was almost two-thirds higher than that for men, and women voters under thirty rated it as highly as their male counterparts.[57]

CARTER IS CANONISED

'If Shakespeare could have written a gangster movie, *Get Carter* would surely be the one.' 'fatglyn', Plymouth (IMDB user comments, 2 June 2001)

Formal rehabilitation of *Get Carter* began with a screening at the NFT in September 1997. Mike Hodges introduced the film and answered questions from the audience. Regular showings of the film followed on the satellite channel, TNT. On Saturday 27 February 1999, TNT gave *Get Carter* a special screening in its correct aspect ratio together with an interview with Michael Caine about the making of the film and its significance. By this time, the success of a new British crime film, *Lock, Stock and Two Smoking Barrels* (Guy Ritchie, 1998) had given *Get Carter* a fresh currency as an inspirational text for a new generation of British directors. Playfully packed full of references to previous British gangster films, *Lock, Stock* ... fetishised the long-barrelled hunting gun used by Carter. The poster for the film showed Vinnie Jones with two matching weapons resting on his shoulders in a pose that seemed a conscious homage to Caine's character. Janet Staiger has noted that film-makers can have a significant influence in the revision of film canons: 'Those films chosen to be reworked, alluded to, satirized, become privileged points of reference [...] As ideal fathers, these select films are given homage or rebelled against.'[58] As a rash of new crime movies, eager to capitalise on the market established by Guy Ritchie, went into production in 1999, *Get Carter* became a totem of a resurgent genre. That each of the new wave of gangster films proved to be artistically inferior to Mike Hodges' effort served only to increase the esteem in which his film was now held.

The BFI finally canonised *Get Carter* by releasing a restored print for cinema exhibition in June 1999. It was first in a string of re-releases of classic British crime films, the others being *The Third Man*, *The Italian Job* and *The Long Good Friday* (John MacKenzie, 1980). Hailing *Carter* as a 'cult classic', the BFI press release described it as 'the best British gangster movie ever made', and acknowledged its historical significance in the way it had, at the beginning of the 1970s, introduced 'an ethos of cynicism directly opposed to the free spirited sixties'. Subsequent thrillers, the press release suggested, remained 'forever in its debt'.[59]

Interest in the re-release was helped by the news in April that the film was to be remade with an American cast. The new producer, Mark Canton, revealed a reverence for the original: 'I'm very respectful of Mike's movie [...] *Get Carter* was a cutting edge picture and we want to keep the character but transfer him to a contemporary New York or Los Angeles setting.'[60] The re-release quickly turned into something of a media event, making the news pages of the broadsheet press before reviews appeared in the film sections. In *The Times*, under the headline 'Tyne trek for *Get Carter* pilgrims', Adam Sherwin pointed to the growing significance of film-based tourism, and suggested that Tyneside might benefit from the popularity of the film in the same way that Sheffield had from *The Full Monty* (Peter Cattaneo, 1997).[61] In spite of the unflattering portrait of Tyneside presented in *Carter*, Fraser Kemp, a local Labour MP and a member of the All-Party Film Group, was reported to be calling for the instigation of an official 'tourist trail'. The film, he said, 'had a dramatic impact on people like me when I was growing up in the north east and we should be encouraging people to visit the locations'. Kemp's idea received the immediate support of minister for tourism and film, Janet Anderson, herself a 'Geordie girl'.[62] Cinematic notoriety, it seemed, might go some way towards compensating for the catastrophic decline of heavy industry in the north.

Get Carter's new publicity carried ringing endorsements from the 'lads' press': 'sadistically captivating and cinematically stylish' (*GQ*), 'British pulp noir at its finest (*Loaded*). The *Guardian*, a paper not previously known for championing the emblems of 'lad culture', for once found itself on the same side as *Loaded* when it began to sing the praises of *Get Carter*, even before the film's re-release. Not content to label his 'seminal' movie 'the toughest, coldest and greatest British gangster film of all time', Tom Cox's double-page feature on Mike Hodges hyperbolically insisted that it was 'bigger than British cinema itself'.[63] Andrew Antony in the *Guardian* called it 'one of the most welcome re-releases in years'. Praising Caine's performance and Hodges' direction, he concluded that, although the film had grown 'a fascinating documentary skin over time', it had not aged.[64] James Christopher in *The Times* suggested that *Get Carter* had 'shattered the mould of breezy British thrillers' and nearly three decades later had 'lost none of its vintage kick'.[65] Alexander Walker, one of the few critics consistently to emphasise the importance of *Get Carter* as a barometer of its times, could now declare, in spite of his misgivings about the film's brutality, that Hodges had created a 'visionary' movie that heralded the breakdown of the old community networks and the arrival of a vicious individualism. 'It showed us what was coming,' he concluded.[66]

The marketing campaign for the re-release deliberately targeted a younger audience, using advertising slots on Kiss FM radio and the standard club promotional techniques of flyposting and the distribution of eye-catching fliers (complete with an endorsement from *Dazed and Confused* magazine). Awareness within club culture was enhanced by the simultaneous release of DJ remixes of Budd's *Get Carter* theme, and a special night at the Wag Club. Opening at seven venues in London, Tyneside and Edinburgh, the film grossed a respectable £16,200 in its first weekend, and went on to gross £124,296.[67]

The measure of *Get Carter*'s re-evaluation was evident a few months later when the BFI published its list of 100 top British films, voted for by members of the film industry and prominent academics. Not only had 'the great and the good' recognised *Get Carter*'s worth by placing it at number 16 in the list, but, after decades of critical exclusion, the crime thriller was finally acknowledged as a key generic component of the national cinema. The repressed gangster movie returned to haunt the top half of the charts, from the number-one film, *The Third Man*, through *Brighton Rock* (15), *The Long Good Friday* (21) and *The Italian Job* (36) to *Performance* at number 48.[68]

As the twenty-first century dawned, the re-released *Get Carter* had almost finished doing the round of regional film theatres, but the buzz around the film showed no sign of abating. A knighthood for Michael Caine added to the growing respectability of the film he regards as his favourite. Steven Soderbergh's new release *The Limey* (2000), the story of a London gangster who travels to Los Angeles to investigate the death of his daughter, owed a clear debt to Mike Hodges' film, even if the footage it incorporated was from *Poor Cow*. In the magazine press, *Esquire*, a publication that had previously remained fairly aloof from its competitors' enthusiasm for the criminal underworld and its filmic representation, ran a guide to British gangsterdom.[69] It was accompanied by eight pages of photographs taken by Wolfgang Suschitzky on location for *Get Carter*. Mike Hodges provided the captions.[70]

In America, where the film has been largely unavailable since its original patchy release, *Get Carter* continued to acquire a deepening mystique – an authentic original glimpsed only through the distorting glass of inferior domestic copies.[71] In the autumn of 2000, *Hit Man* was joined by Stephen Kay's lacklustre reworking of Hodges' classic. The new film paid homage to the original in the ironic casting of Michael Caine as Brumby, and in renaming Glenda after the actress who played her in Hodges' film, Geraldine (Moffat). More British acting talent in the shape of Alan Cumming as Kinnear and Miranda Richardson as Gloria (the widow of Carter's brother) linked the remake to its roots. David MacKenna's script, however, is like one of those carefully numbered pieces of British architectural heritage painstakingly shipped to the New World only to be reassembled with the doors where the windows should be and the whole thing facing in the wrong direction. Whereas *Hit Man* had remained generally faithful to the characterisations and narrative of the original, MacKenna revels in deconstruction and mutation. While some of the changes – like the transformation of Kinnear into a nerdy computer software tycoon – offer a potentially interesting update, most are at best gratuitous.[72] At worst, they are motivated by a desire to legitimise Carter and soften the social critique that gives Hodges' film its political depth and resonance.

Although Kay saturates his *mise-en-scène* with rain, and de-saturates its colour, he is unable to pass his film off as a noir tragedy. As a post-Tarantino crime movie protagonist, Sylvester Stallone's reconstructed Carter can barely be classed as an anti-hero. He may remain capable of killing villains (even of shooting them in the back), but he is well on the road to spiritual redemption, remorseful about his shirking of family duties, polite, capable of mercy, sexually continent and sensitive in his dealings with women. His adversary, the internet pornographer Cyrus Paice (Mickey Rourke playing Eric, but in much better shape) even has to remind him: 'You're the bad brother, remember?' For this Carter, the return home to Seattle is not the end of the road but a rediscovery of the righteous path. Whereas Caine's Carter remained largely an enigma, a sign for something more elemental than the self, Stallone's is engaged in an active exploration of his identity. The ultimate moment of epiphany comes when he tearfully comforts his bereaved niece (no ambiguity about his relationship to Doreen this time) and reassures her: 'We can't change our history, but we can go past it.' Like the exchange between Carter and Margaret in the original, the conversation with Doreen (Rachel Leigh Cook) takes place in an elevated setting, but this time there is no hint of irony. The roof where they forge their family bond and Carter discovers that 'the truth hurts', really does represent a moral high ground. In this context, Carter's mission of revenge becomes almost a penance for past sins. Certainly, Kay does his best to dismiss Brumby's contention that 'revenge doesn't work' and to support Carter's retort that 'sure it does'. Kay uses the techniques Hodges eventually rejected – brief flashbacks to the murder of Carter's brother and rape of his niece – to justify his protagonist's killings, which he also allows to go unpunished. By the time that he has discovered that the real villain of the piece is not snivelling Kinnear, but the duplicitous Brumby, he has also learned to see his own life of crime as futile and spiritually empty. When he finally bids goodbye to Doreen, he has shaved off the satanic goatee he has sported all through the film, as if to confirm that Hollywood productions will always prefer optimism to pessimism and conventional sentiment to moral ambiguity.

Even with all its high-octane car chases, impressionistic jump cuts and expressionistic camera techniques, Kay's modish dub version of *Get Carter* failed to inspire a following. It was so poorly received in the USA that Warner Bros. chose not to release the film for theatrical exhibition in Britain, where among the ranks of reviewers, fans of the original were eagerly sharpening their knives in anticipation. Kay was well aware of what the reception would be like: 'We're going to get crushed in London. It's tantamount to a British film-maker remaking *Mean Streets*.'[73] UK consumers who had gone to the expense of importing the American DVD were likely to echo one of Michael Caine's last lines in the film: 'What a mess, eh? All over a shiny piece of plastic.' More than eighteen months after its première, the film went straight to video/DVD rental in Carter's homeland.

In October 2000, with the remake in American cinemas, and Hodges' sleeper movie, *Croupier* (1999) doing good business on the art-house circuit, Warner Bros. released a digitally remastered *Get Carter* for the first time on DVD and in widescreen video. The movie was accompanied by its American trailer, footage of Roy Budd playing the theme tune, and Caine's filmed introduction for the Newcastle première, with additional commentary by Hodges, Caine and Suschitzky. Warner's marketeers pulled out all the stops, offering a limited-edition run in 'luxury film cases' with a copy of the screenplay and four collectors' images, and ballyhooing the release with full-page advertising in the film monthlies

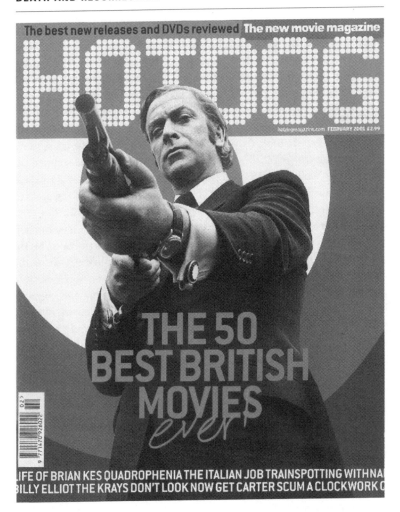

18. *Gangster No. 1. The Carter icon dominates the cover of* Hotdog, *February 2001.*

and point-of-sale displays in retail outlets. MGM's previous releases of *Get Carter* on video had conformed to the standard practice, for films of this vintage, of presenting it as part of a series, but Warner Bros. decided to promote the film as if it were new product. Rejecting the multiplicity of images with which the film had been promoted in the past, the new release used the BFI poster to establish a single icon for *Get Carter*: the *National Heroes* publicity photograph of Caine levelling a pump-action shotgun – presumably a more familiar gangster's weapon to American audiences than the long-barrelled gun actually used on screen. *Total Film* carried four pages of promotion and 'advertorial' on the film, and the newcomer to the monthly film press, *Hotdog*, featured an interview with Mike Hodges to go with its five-star review and recommendation for purchase.[74] *Later* (*Loaded*'s more thoroughbred stablemate at IPC magazines) went one better by running a five-page article on the making of *Get Carter*.[75] It took its place in the magazine's 'nostalgia' section, even though few of *Later*'s readers were born when Caine stepped off the ferry at Wallsend. *Empire* followed suit with its own five-page article on the 'Number One Gangster'.[76] The impetus provided by the scale of its release took the new-look, new-format, added-value *Get Carter* to number three in the DVD sales charts and straight into the video top ten, even though some retailers had only recently cleared its previous MGM version from their sale shelves. On 9 November 2000, in the wake of the DVD release and with the British première of Stephen Kay's remake imminent, BBC Television's *Film 2000* decided the time had come to 'celebrate what is probably the greatest British gangster movie of them all'. As well as footage of the *Get Carter* Appreciation Society restaging scenes from the film, and extracts from a 1970 BBC Newcastle *Look North* report on the making of Hodges' movie, the piece contained the extraordinary sight of Sylvester Stallone appealing to Gateshead Council to save Cliff Brumby's car park from demolition. To presenter Jonathan Ross's comment, that *Get Carter* 'redrew the boundaries of the gangster film', we might equally add 'and is redrawing the boundaries of a legitimate national cinema'. Mike Hodges' 'unflinchingly brutal master-piece' now really is established as 'a Brit classic'.[77] *Hotdog* magazine was sufficiently carried away with the euphoria of *Carter*'s re-evaluation to award it the top spot in its '50 Best British Movies Ever'.[78]

Get Carter's transformation, in the space of less than a decade, from an old crime film to an honoured part of the heritage of British cinema is evidence of a changed frame of reference in our evaluation of the past. The conception of nationhood and national character that the British cinema canon has always reflected seems to have swelled to encompass the sordid and sensational as well as the saintly and sober. 'The side of Britain that people didn't want to see' has now become a source of nostalgic interest, a concrete car park in search of a preservation order. At the same time, the ability of genre cinema to reproduce the appearances of everyday life, and to move audiences by the power of its narrative drive, at last appears to have received legitimation. What ultimately makes *Carter*'s critical recuperation easier than most other examples of its genre, however, is its particular affinities with respectable traditions of British drama: the role of tragedy in the theatre, and social realism in the cinema.

CONCLUDING *CARTER*

'At last vengeance has come into my hands, and come, indeed, entire.' Seneca, *Thyestes*, II.494–5[79]

The beach is deserted. The coal-black waves no longer lap at Carter's forehead. The bottle launched by Hodges in another age has been found and the prophetic spirit within has been uncorked. Like some wronged Jacobean spectre, the spirit has haunted the halls of British film culture. But now *Carter*'s revenge is complete because it extends beyond the text into the citadel of film criticism itself. The film, and the outcast genre it exemplifies, has returned home in legitimation.

Get Carter's rehabilitation raises intriguing questions about the changing climate of audience spectatorship and critical reception. What does it say about new institutional strategies of interpretation? Which groups and what practices now influence admission to the canon of British cinema? Is three decades a safe distance from which to view the film's ugly violence and disturbing gender politics? Is *Carter* no longer to be condemned for its masochistic positioning of the female spectator, but rather read 'against the grain' as a parable of patriarchal domination? Is it now, like the Jacobean revenger's tragedy, to be enjoyed as a historical piece that captures the structures of feeling of its period? Or is *Carter* even to be openly celebrated for its aesthetic display of masculine individualist performance?

There is no doubt that *Get Carter* has been buffeted by the ebb and flow of gender politics, and the mid-1990s reassertion of pride in masculinity can go some way towards accounting for its changing critical fortunes. The reasons for its growing resonance with young audiences, however, extend beyond discourses of gender.

First, *Carter* has benefited from the cultural transformations set in motion by Tarantino's *Reservoir Dogs* and *Pulp Fiction*. Taking their cues from the exploitation films of the 1970s, these gangster-centred narratives remodelled attitudes towards the professional criminal. Violent crime was explicitly constructed as a form of work and the gangster was portrayed as an ordinary person with ordinary (and by extension) legitimate desires. The mundanities of everyday conversation and cultural reference were carefully fetishised in a way that encouraged spectator identification and the suspension of moral judgement. The work ethic was ironically deployed to efface the differences between legitimate and illegitimate labour, leaving the audience free to appreciate the 'cool' persona of the professional killer with a minimum of guilt. With this retuning of sensibilities, onscreen killing became an aesthetic rather than an ethical issue, part of the work a cinematic hitman must do to gratify audiences more interested in the minutiae of style and narrative than in moral lessons. As a protagonist, the fastidious Jack Carter, with his caustic one-liners, unflappable composure and detached attitude to murder, was ideally attuned to the sensibilities developed by Tarantino. Carter's apparent devotion to his dead brother also fitted well with the system of loyalty promoted in Tarantino's cinema: the elevation of male friendship above social responsibility and fidelity to the law. Hodges admits to being mildly puzzled and perturbed by this turn of events. As he once confessed: 'To be honest, when I was making it, I thought no one would want to see this film because it is so horrendous.'[80]

Second, *Get Carter*'s revival was facilitated by a renewed interest in British film following the success of *Four Weddings and a Funeral* (Mike Newell, 1994) and *Trainspotting*. Danny Boyle's film, in particular, signified to the multiplex generation that an indigenous cinema could be as exciting and stylish as Hollywood's products, and that it was capable of producing stars as well as actors. Just as lads' mags like *Loaded* had validated indigenous and well-established male lifestyles, so the succession of 'Cool Britannia' movies that followed *Trainspotting* cultivated a taste for ethnocentric cultural representations that challenged Hollywood's hegemony. Satisfying this appetite for hip dramas located in an authentic British milieu proved to be a task beyond most directors, even with the influx of lottery funding, but there were enough successes to keep the appetite whetted. In these conditions, *Get Carter* began to be looked to as a benchmark of both style and authenticity, a film that set the standard for dry humour and icy nihilism and managed to invest British locations with the kind of shabby exoticism strived for by Danny Boyle and Guy Ritchie.

Third, *Get Carter*'s theme of an angry individual taking revenge against those who had wronged him chimed with the mood of audiences emerging from a decade of ruthless Thatcherite policies to revelations about government sleaze and corruption. In Hodges' view, his film began to fit more comfortably with the view of themselves held by the British:

19. *A bottle of whisky swallowed neat before breakfast.* Get Carter
supplies a tonic to the British film canon.

'When the film came out, we had a totally hypocritical view of what life
in Britain was like, but I think that now that has all been stripped away
and you cannot deny that, like everywhere else, corruption is endemic.'[81]
In the gangsters' paradise which many felt Britain had become by the
mid-1990s, Carter's crusade took on a fresh allegorical significance.
Carter embodied the cold anger and frustrated yearnings for revenge
that ensured the defeat of the Conservative Party at the 1997 election.

Like Jack, those disadvantaged by eighteen years of Tory 'reforms' needed to kick ass, and in a political culture in which the power of collective action had been emasculated, his wild individualism may have seemed highly appropriate. As a revenger, he was certainly a more formidable figure than Tony Blair.

Finally, *Get Carter* displays a prime criterion of success in the post-modern film marketplace: the ability to offer multiple points of access to diverse audiences. Recent film theory has stressed the ways in which popular movies are designed in an almost modular fashion to incorporate points of appeal to different potential audiences. These textual elements become integral parts of subsequent marketing strategies.[82] With *Carter*, this is not so much a premeditated strategy as a post hoc development. As we have seen, the film was originally marketed on the basis of genre and star persona, but alternative routes into the movie have subsequently opened up. Although, for many women, the routes remain blocked by Carter's misogyny, others can find ways in via a love of 1970s style, an affection for the north east, or the sexual appeal of the domineering male. And then there are the 'imperilled traces' of a vanishing world, and the idiosyncrasies of personal biography that make films significant to the individual. We must also add the polysemic complexion of the film's politics. For one admirer, the *New Statesman*'s critic Jonathan Coe, *Carter*'s virtue is its 'radical simplicity' as 'one of the least literary films ever made in this country'. It apparently carries 'absolutely no verbal, intellectual or ideological baggage'. Instead, it is a film of 'primal emotions and elemental power' in which the protagonist has probably never had a political thought enter his head.[83] While, for Alexander Walker, *Carter* is a politically 'visionary' movie that warns of corruption yet to be uncovered and social dissolution yet to come.[84] Beneath the apparent simplicity of *Get Carter*'s relentless narrative of self-destruction is the buried story of a society bent on a similar course. It may not be a universal story for all people at all times, but it is a compelling story for some people at some times. When those times become an indelible historical moment, a cult can become a classic.

APPENDIX
Scene Breakdown and Shooting Schedule

The breakdown below is based on the 30 June 1970 revision of *Carter's the Name*, the scene breakdown for *Carter* produced on 16 July 1970 by assistant director Keith Evans, the (incomplete) call sheets and movement orders issued by Evans and location manager Derek Gibson during filming, and the post-production script for *Get Carter*. Scenes omitted from the final cut of *Get Carter* are indicated in *italics*. Scenes added during location filming are indicated by an asterisk (*).

20. *On location: Mike Hodges directs one of* Get Carter's *pub scenes.*

Scene	Location	Description	Filmed	Comments
1	*Ext. Suburban street*	*Establishing shot of Carter at window of Fletchers' Victorian house*		*Not filmed*
1a*	Int. Fletchers' penthouse	Crane shot through window	20.7.70	Substituted
2	Int. Fletchers' penthouse	Porn slide show	20.7.70	Revoiced for USA
3	Ext. Train	Travelling north	17.9.70	2nd unit
4	Int. Train compartment	Carter reads novel		
5	Ext. Countryside from train	Travelling north		2nd unit
6	Int. Train corridor	Carter on train	21.7.70	
7	Ext. Countryside from train	Travelling north		2nd unit
8	Int. Train toilet	Carter takes pills	17.9.70	2nd unit
9	Ext. Train	Travelling north		2nd unit
10	Int. Train restaurant car	Carter cleans spoon	21.7.70	
11	Ext. Newcastle from train	Train pulls into station	21.7.70	
12	Int. Newcastle station	Carter walks down platform	22.7.70	
13	*Int. Newcastle station*	*Carter waits at left luggage*	22.7.70	*Not used*
14	*Ext. Newcastle station*	*Carter seen leaving station by one-legged paper seller*	22.7.70	*Not used*
15	Int. North Eastern bar	Carter enters bar and orders pint	22.7.70	
16	*Ext. Newcastle station*	*Paper seller leaves his stand*	22.7.70	*Not used*
17	Int. North Eastern bar	Carter receives phone call	22.7.70	
18	*Ext. Newcastle station*	*Paper seller goes to taxi kiosk*	22.7.70	*Not used*
19	Int. North Eastern bar	Carter on phone	22.7.70	
20	*Ext. Newcastle station*	*Taxi controller on telephone*	22.7.70	*Not used*
21	Int. North Eastern bar	Carter speaks to Margaret on phone	22.7.70	
22	*Ext. North Eastern bar*	*Carter leaves bar*		*Not used*
23	*Ext. Newcastle station*	*Carter hires a car*		*Not used*

Scene	Location	Description	Filmed	Comments
51	Int. Crematorium	Coffin burns	25.7.70	
52	Ext. Crematorium	Carter talks to Margaret	25.7.70	
53	Ext. Crematorium	Child's cortege arrives	25.7.70	
54	Int. Half Moon pub	Mourners discuss Frank. Doreen throws drink at Eddie	c. 28.7.70	
55	Int. Fletchers' bedroom	Anna on telephone	20.7.70	*Not used*
56	Ext. Half Moon	Carter on telephone to Anna		*Not used*
57	Int. Fletchers' bedroom	Anna on telephone	20.7.70	*Not used*
58	Ext. Half Moon	Carter on telephone		*Not used*
59	Int. Fletchers' bedroom	Anna on telephone	20.7.70	*Not used*
60	Ext. Half Moon	Carter sees two suspicious men enter pub		*Not used*
61	Int. Half Moon	Men question bar staff		*Not used*
62	Ext. Half Moon	Men spot Carter and chase him		*Not used*
63	Int. Large store	Carter attempts to fool men tailing him		*Not filmed*
64	Int. Photographic machine	Carter hides from pursuers		*Not filmed*
65	Ext. Large store	Pursuers leave store		*Not filmed*
66	Int. Large store	Carter leaves photo booth		*Not filmed*
67	Ext. Large store	Men have lost Carter		*Not filmed*
68	Int. Hire car	Carter looking for the car in which his brother died		*Not filmed*
69	Ext. River bank	Carter finds car, with boys fishing nearby		*Not filmed*
69a	Ext. Scrapyard	Carter finds car	12.9.70	Substituted and repositioned
70–83	Ext. Newcastle racecourse	Carter looks for Albert at races, but finds Eric		Scenes originally included Kinnear
84	Int. Hire car	Carter tails Eric's Cadillac		
85	Int. Cadillac	Driving to 'The Heights'		
86	Int. Hire car	Carter watches Cadillac arrive at 'The Heights'		

Scene	Location	Description	Filmed	Comments
111a*	Ext. Dance hall	Carter follows Thorpe into dance hall	10.9.70	Additional scene
112	Int. Dance hall	Carter catches Thorpe and starts a brawl	10.9.70	Brawl deleted
113	Int. Dance hall toilet	Carter corners Thorpe	10.9.70	
114	Ext. Street	Carter takes Thorpe back to Las Vegas		
115	Int. Las Vegas hall	Carter returns with Thorpe		
116	Int. Las Vegas bedroom	Interrogation of Thorpe		
117	Ext. 'The Pantiles'	Carter observes party at Brumby's home		
118	Int. 'The Pantiles'	Brumby ejects party guests		
119	Ext. 'The Pantiles'	Carter enters house		
120	Int. 'The Pantiles'	Carter argues with Brumby		
121	Ext. Las Vegas	Carter returns to Las Vegas		
122	Int. Las Vegas hall	Carter enters cautiously		
123	Int. Las Vegas sitting room	Carter talks to Edna and her purple underwear is revealed		
123a*	Ext. Las Vegas	Girls' marching band		Additional scene
124	Int. Las Vegas bedroom	Enda brings Carter breakfast in bed. Con and Peter intrude on their love-making. Carter ejects them at gunpoint		Breakfast deleted, scene split up
124a*	Ext. Las Vegas	Marching band		Additional scene
124b*	Ext. Las Vegas	Con and Peter arrive in Jag		Additional scene
125	Ext. Las Vegas	Carter walks into street naked		
126	Int. Las Vegas bedroom	Carter dresses		
127	Ext. Las Vegas back alley	Carter locks Con in toilet		
128	Ext. Back alley	Carter drives through washing		
129	Ext. Las Vegas	Jaguar's door ripped off		

130	Ext. Riverside	Carter parks car at bottom of Tyne Bridge and takes lift	10.8.70	Not used
131	Ext. Tyne Bridge	Carter loses pursuing Jaguar and walks over bridge	10.8.70	Not used
132	Ext. Back street	Carter arrives at Keith's house	15.9.70	Originally on foot
133	Int. Keith's hall	Carter enters house		Exterior shot used
134	Int. Keith's room	Carter talks to injured Keith		
135	Ext. Riverside	Ferry docking	8.8.70	
136	Ext. Ferry	Carter on ferry. Passengers include boy dressed as cowboy	8.8.70	Repositioned (163a)
137	Ext. Jetty	Albert spots Carter as he drives off ferry	8.8.70	Not used
138	Ext. Caravan site	Carter looks for Albert	7.9.70	Location changed to cafe. Not used
139	Int. Albert's caravan	Carter questions Albert's girlfriend	7.9.70	Location changed to cafe. Not used
140	Ext. High Level Bridge	Carter meets Margaret. They are interrupted by Con and Peter	?/10.8.70	
141	Ext. Below bridge	Carter runs from Con and Peter	10/15.8.70	
142	Ext. Riverside	Carter is picked up by Glenda	10/15.8.70	
143	Int. Glenda's car	Driving to car park		
144	Int. Car park	Entering car park		
145	Int. Penthouse restaurant	Brumby tells Carter that Kinnear killed his brother		
146	Int. Car park	Carter picked up by Glenda as he leaves		
147	Cross cuts: Int. Glenda's car / Int. Glenda's bedroom	Glenda driving cross cut with Glenda and Carter having sex	12.9.70 / ?	
147a*	Ext. Tower block	Establishing shot of Glenda's block of flats	12.9.70	Additional scene
148	Int. Glenda's bedroom	Carter and Glenda talk in bed		
149	Int. Glenda's bathroom	Glenda in bath		
150	Int. Glenda's bedroom	Carter watches Doreen in porn film		
151	The blue movie	Glenda and Margaret prepare Doreen for Albert's arrival	Before 17.7.70	
152	Int. Glenda's bathroom	Carter roughs up Glenda		
153	Ext. Tower block	Carter locks Glenda in car boot	10.8.70	

Scene	Location	Description	Filmed	Comments
154	Ext. Ferry jetty	Carter drives off ferry	8.8.70	
155	Ext. Caravan site	Carter looks for Albert. Albert's girlfriend makes phone call		Not filmed
155a*	Int. Cafe	Carter questions Albert's girlfriend	7.9.70	Substitute scene
156	Int. Albert's caravan	Carter looks for Albert		Not filmed
157	Ext. Hillside South Shields	Looking for Albert		Not filmed
157a*	Ext. Back street	Carter walks to bookmaker's while Albert's girlfriend phones	7.9.70	Substitute scene
158	Ext. Caravan site	Albert's girlfriend on phone	7.9.70	Location changed to cafe. Used as voiceover
159	Ext. Pigeon allotment	Carter finds Albert and questions him		Not filmed
159a*	Int. Betting shop	Carter finds Albert	7.9.70	Substitute scene
160	Int. Albert's caravan	Subliminal shot of Frank's murder – forced to drink whisky		Not filmed
161	Ext. Pigeon allotment	Carter stabs Albert and takes his binoculars		Not filmed
161a*	Ext. Betting shop backyard	Carter stabs Albert	7.9.70	Substitute scene
161b*	Int. Betting shop	Carter leaves	7.9.70	Additional scene
162	Ext. Ferry road	Carter, chased by gangsters, ditches Glenda's car from jetty	8.8.70	Not used
163	Ext. Top Road	Flashback of Frank's car being ditched		Not filmed
163a	Int. Ferry	Carter watches other passengers	8.8.70	Repositioned from 136
164	Ext. Jetty	Carter and gangsters take cover	8.8.70	Incorporated into 164a
164a*	Ext. Jetty	Ferry docks	8.8.70	Substitute scene
165	Ext. River bank	Subliminal flashback of Jack and Frank as young men with their shotgun		Not filmed

166–68	Ext. Jetty/Ext. Waiting room	Cross cut gun fight	8.8.70	Ferry location substituted for jetty
169	*Ext. Beach*	*Subliminal shot of Carter and Anna making love on a beach*		*Not filmed*
170	Ext. Waiting room	Carter shoots Peter, who falls into water	8.8.70	Ferry location substituted
171	*Int. Fletcher's bedroom*	*Subliminal shot of Anna's face being slashed*	*20.7.70*	*Not used*
172	Ext. Jetty	Con and Peter leave, pursued by police	8.8.70	Scene adapted to incorporate Glenda's death
173	*Ext. Riverside*	*Carter finds car and drives off*		*Not filmed*
173a*	Ext. Car park	Carter drives into car park	12.9.70	Substitute scene
174	Int. Penthouse restaurant	Brumby talks to architects. They hear Carter arrive	11.9.70	
175	Ext. Car park stairs	Brumby investigates. Carter hits Brumby	11.9.70	
176	*Int. Albert's bedroom*	*Subliminal flashback of Albert and Doreen about to have sex*	*Before 17.7.70*	*Not used*
177	Ext. Car park	Brumby falls	11.9.70	Landing on car added
178	Int. Hire car	Carter drives off as police arrive	12.9.70	Exterior shot used
179	Int. Penthouse restaurant	Designers discuss fees	11.9.70	
180	Int. Post office	Carter telephones and mails film to Vice Squad		
181	Ext. Swing Bridge	Carter buys drugs	15.9.70	
182	*Int. Pub*	*Carter looks for Margaret*		*Not filmed*
183	*Ext. Fishing quay*	*Carter talks to fishermen about Margaret*		*Not filmed*
184	*Ext. Cul-de-sac*	*Carter questions Margaret's friend*	*10.9.70*	*Not used*
185	Int. Bingo hall	Carter locates Margaret	10.9.70	
186	Ext. Bingo hall	Carter follows Margaret and friend	10.9.70	
187	Ext. Fishing quay	Carter trails Margaret	10.9.70	Location changed to back street
188	Ext. River walk	Carter corners Margaret	10.9.70	Location changed to back alley
189	Int. 'The Heights' sitting room	Kinnear goes to phone		
190	Ext. Village telephone box	Carter telephones Kinnear	9.9.70	
191	Int. 'The Heights' sitting room	Kinnear listens		

Scene	Location	Description	Filmed	Comments
192	Ext. telephone box	Carter proposes a deal	9.9.70	
193	Int. 'The Heights' library	Kinnear speaks to Eric		
194	Int. Hire car	Carter drives to wood	9.9.70	Exterior shot used
195	Int. 'The Heights' library	Kinnear telephones hitman		
196	Int. Hotel bedroom	Hitman accepts contract on Carter		
197	Ext. Deserted wood	Carter drives through wood		Repositioned (195)
198	Int./Ext. Hire car	Carter kills Margaret		Repositioned (195)
199	Ext. Country road	Carter watches 'The Heights' through Albert's binoculars. Eric leaves		No binoculars
200	Ext. Phone box	Carter phones police		Voiceover substituted in 199
201	Ext. 'The Heights'	Police arrive and surround house	9.9.70	
202	Ext. Country road	Carter sets off after Eric	9.9.70	
203	Int./Ext. 'The Heights'	Police raid house and find Margaret's body in grounds		
204	Ext. 'The Heights'	Kinnear arrested		
205	Int./Ext. Hire Car	Carter drives to Jetty	15.9.70	
206	Ext. Coal jetty	Carter chases Eric	15.9.70	
206a	Ext. 'The Heights'/Ext. Jetty	Cross cuts between chase and police raid	?/15.9.70	
207	Ext. Beach	Chase continues		
208	Ext. Beach	Eric stumbles		
209	Ext. Beach	Carter catches Eric and kills him		
210	Ext. Beach	Eric's body is bundled into cable car and dumped into sea		
211	Ext. Cliff top	Hitman 'J' shoots Carter		
212	Ext. Beach	Carter lies dead		

Notes

1. *CARTER* IN CONTEXT

1. Chibnall and Murphy (eds), *British Crime Cinema*, p. 121.
2. Janet Staiger, 'The Politics of Film Canons', *Cinema Journal*, 24, 1985, p. 17.
3. Umberto Eco, *The Name of the Rose*, New York: Warner Books, 1984, p. 79.
4. For a discussion on the textual properties of cult films, see the contributions to J. P. Telotte (ed.), *The Cult Film Experience: Beyond All Reason*, Austin: University of Texas Press, 1991.
5. A similarity to the western is noted, for example, by Billson, *My Name is Michael Caine*, p. 79.
6. Of course, it is also a scenario familiar from the Samurai cinema of Akira Kurosawa, on whose *Yojimbo* (1961) Leone based *For a Few Dollars More*.
7. William Shakespeare, *King Lear* (1605), IV.ii.49.
8. Albert Camus, *Selected Essays and Notebooks*, Harmondsworth: Penguin, 1970, p. 194.
9. Gamini Salgado, 'Introduction', *Three Jacobean Tragedies*, Harmondsworth: Penguin, 1965.
10. Hodges quoted in Darke, 'From Gangland to the Casino Table'.
11. See Robert Murphy, *Sixties British Cinema*, London: BFI, 1992, pp. 139–60; Bruce Carson, 'Comedy, Sexuality and "Swinging London" Films', *Journal of Popular British Cinema*, 1, 1998, pp. 50–59.
12. John Grierson quoted in Kathryn Dodd and Philip Dodd, 'Engendering the Nation: British Documentary Film', in A. Higson (ed.), *Dissolving Views: Key Writings on British Cinema*, London: Cassell, 1996, pp. 38–50.
13. Andrew Higson, *Waving the Flag: Constructing a National Cinema in Britain*, Oxford: Oxford University Press, 1995, pp. 190–91.
14. M. L. Jennings (ed.), *Humphrey Jennings: Painter, Poet, Film-maker*, London: BFI, 1982.
15. *The Guardian*, 28 May 1999.
16. Hall, *Raising Caine*, p. 171.
17. Salgado, *Three Jacobean Tragedies*, p. 20.
18. '*Scelera non ulcisceris, nisi vincis.*'
19. Michael Caine interviewed in *Loaded*, 58, February 1999.
20. Jonathan Dollimore, *Radical Tragedy*, Brighton: Harvester, 1984, p. 50.
21. Ibid.
22. Hodges quoted in Neil Spencer, 'The Caine Mutiny', *Uncut*, June 1998, pp. 31–3.
23. TNT, 27 February 1999.

24. Hodges quoted in Tom Dewe Mathews, 'Now Get the Son of *Get Carter*', *Evening Standard*, 11 June 1999, pp. 34–5.

25. See J. P. Telotte (ed.), *The Cult Film Experience*, particularly the essays in 'Introduction: Mapping the Cult'. It is also worth noting V. F. Perkins' more general comment that, 'Films can make us associate with attitudes which are not our own, with thoughts, feelings and actions which are outside our normal range' (*Film as Film*, Harmondsworth: Penguin, 1988, p. 138).

26. Dollimore, *Radical Tragedy*, p. 149.

27. J. W. Lever, *The Tragedy of State*, London: Methuen, 1971, p. 10.

28. *Photoplay*, May 1971.

29. Hall, *Raising Caine*, p. 171.

30. Quoted in Paul Duncan, 'All the Way Home: Ted Lewis', *Crime Time*, 9, 1997, p. 25.

31. Ibid., pp. 22–6.

32. Murphy, 'A Revenger's Tragedy – *Get Carter*', in Chibnall and Murphy (eds), *British Crime Cinema*, p. 125.

33. Lewis, *Jack's Return Home*, pp. 7, 21.

34. Ibid., p. 167.

35. Ibid., p. 170.

36. One might go further to suggest that Carter's dead brother represented the lack felt by Lewis as an only child.

37. Duncan, 'All the Way Home', p. 22.

38. Ibid., p. 23.

39. George Orwell, 'Raffles and Miss Blandish' (1944), in the *Collected Essays, Journalism and Letters of George Orwell: Volume 3*, Harmondsworth: Penguin, 1968, pp. 246–60.

40. Richard Hoggart, *The Uses of Literacy*, London: Chatto and Windus, 1957.

41. Steve Chibnall, *Making Mischief: The Cult Films of Pete Walker*, Guildford: FAB Press, 1998, p. 66.

42. Robert Murphy, *Sixties British Cinema*, London: BFI, 1992, pp. 265–7.

43. Gallagher, *Candidly Caine*, pp. 126–7.

44. Hodges quoted in Adams, *Mike Hodges*, p. 14.

45. Hodges, sleevenotes to *Get Carter: An Original Soundtrack Recording*, Chessington: Castle, 1998.

46. Hodges quoted in Adams, *Mike Hodges*, p. 16.

47. In Lewis's novel Carter is alone in his carriage, and the slight indications of impending violence and death feature Carter as the agent of destruction: '*Penthouse* was dead. I'd killed the *Standard* twice' (*Jack's Return Home*, p. 5).

48. The outcry these films provoked on release is described in Walker, *National Heroes*, pp. 40–46. Hodges was asked to take over on *Straw Dogs* when Peckinpah became ill (*Neon*, September 1997, p. 99).

49. Hodges, 'Getting Carter … ', p. 20.

50. Hodges quoted in Adams, *Mike Hodges*, p. 22.

51. Ibid.

52. In Lewis's novel, Carter's first encounter with Eric and his assignation with Margaret are in a pub. The deaths of Albert and Peter take place at Albert Swift's run-down cottage, and Carter goes to buy heroin in Grimsby.

53. Hodges, sleevenotes for *Get Carter: An Original Soundtrack Recording*.

54. Quoted in Dewe Mathews, 'Now Get the Son of *Get Carter*', pp. 34–5.

55. Freedland, *Michael Caine*, pp. 209–10.

56. Ibid., p. 213.

57. Mike Hodges, personal communication with the author, 29 April 2002.

58. *Loaded*, February 1999.

59. US Press Book, MGM, 1971.

60. Ibid.

61. UK Press Book, MGM/EMI, 1971.

62. DVD commentary.

63. US Press Book.

64. Gidney, *Street Life*, p. 127.

65. Ibid., p. 129.

66. For further information on Bindon, see Mick Brown, *Performance*, London: Bloomsbury, 1999, pp. 21–3.

67. Personal communication with the author, 29 April 2002.

68. Quoted in Gidney, *Street Life*, p. 128.

69. *Kinematograph Weekly*, 18 July 1970.

70. Newcastle-upon-Tyne's *Journal*, 8 September 1970.

71. Hodges quoted in Hodgkinson, 'The Making of *Get Carter*', p. 57.

72. www.mbspecial.worldonline.co.uk/getcarter/extras/eileen.htm

73. *Evening Chronicle*, 22 July 1970.

74. La Frenais quoted in Gallagher, *Candidly Caine*, p. 129.

75. Caine, *What's It All About*, p. 323.

76. Klinger quoted in Gallagher, *Candidly Caine*, p. 129.

77. Freedland, *Michael Caine*, p. 215.

78. *Evening Chronicle*, 22 July 1970.

79. *Journal*, 25 July 1970. In addition to the Royal Station Hotel, the production unit also used the Royal Turk's Head in Grey Street; the County Hotel, Neville Street; and the Swallow Hotel, where Mike Hodges stayed. The film's production office was at 35, The Close.

80. *Journal*, 8 September 1970.

81. Ibid.

82. *ABC Film Review*, May 1971, p. 35.

83. Hodges, sleevenotes for *Get Carter*.

84. After *Soldier Blue* (Ralph Nelson, 1970).

85. Paul Fishman, sleevenotes for *Get Carter*.

86. Government Central Office of Information film *Peacemakers*, 1969.

87. Wilf Burns quoted in *T. Dan Smith*, Amber Productions, 1987.

88. Tom Milne, *No Shining Armour*, London: John Calder, 1976, p. 39.

89. Ibid., p. 85.

90. Quoted in Steve Chibnall and Peter Saunders, 'Worlds Apart: Notes on the Social Reality of Corruption', *The British Journal of Sociology*, 28 (2), 1977, p. 143.

91. *Neon*, September 1997, p. 99.

92. John Pearson, *A Profession of Violence*, London: Panther, 1973, p. 158.

93. Eric Mason, *The Inside Story*, London: Pan Books, 1994, p. 174.

94. Reg Kray recalled encountering Stafford again in 1968 while they were both in Brixton Prison, commenting, 'all these years later Ron and I had not forgotten this slight by Dennis Stafford' (Reg Kray, *A Way of Life*, London: Sidgwick and Jackson, 2000, p. 5).

95. Ron Kray with Fred Dinenage, *My Story*, London: Pan Books, 1994, p. 39.

96. David Lewis and Peter Hughman, *Most Unnatural: An Inquiry into the Stafford Case*, Harmondsworth: Penguin, 1971, p. 41.

97. *Secret History*: 'The Porn King, the Stripper and the Bent Coppers', Channel 4, 18 May 1998.

98. Barry Cox, John Shirley and Martin Short, *The Fall of Scotland Yard*, Harmondsworth: Penguin, 1977, p. 166.

99. According to Pearson, *A Profession of Violence*, p. 209, the Krays' firm had ventured into the business of 'protecting' wholesalers and distributors of porn in 1967, but it was difficult for them to make headway in a business that was already thoroughly protected by the OPS.

100. The organisation and eventual exposure of pornography and police corruption in Soho is described in Gilbert Kelland, *Crime in London*, London: Grafton Books, 1987, pp. 160–217; Cox, Shirley and Short, *The Fall of Scotland Yard*, pp. 140–220; and Martin Tomkinson, *The Pornbrokers: The Rise of the Soho Sex Barons*, London: Virgin, 1982, pp. 11–106.

101. Chibnall, *Making Mischief*, pp. 34–7.

102. David Flint, *Babylon Blue*, London: Creation, 1999, pp. 95–7.

103. Lindsay eventually founded his own cinema club, the Taboo, to show his films, surviving two prosecutions after the fall of the OPS before finally being gaoled in the 1980s. For more on Lindsay, see Flint, *Babylon Blue*, pp. 95–7; David McGillivray, *Doing Rude Things*, London: Sun Tavern Fields, 1992.

104. *Sunday Mirror*, 18 May 1975.

105. *Sunday People*, 6 February 1972.

106. Hodges quoted in Spencer, 'The Caine Mutiny', p. 33. For accounts of the Yorkshire police scandals see James Morton, *Bent Coppers*, London: Warner Books, 1994, pp. 122–9.

2. FROM LONDON LUXURY TO TERMINAL BEACH

1. Hodges, *Carter's the Name*, scene 1. The scene was filmed at a fourth-floor apartment in the Quadrangle, Southwick Street, London WC2.

2. Carter's response in the pre-production script was to dismiss the police as 'wankers' (*Carter's the Name*, scene 2).

3. 'J' was not present on the journey in the pre-production script.

4. Hodges had already used a visual *memento mori* in introducing Hunter, the doomed protagonist of his television film *Rumour* (1970). As he drives along London's Westway in his pink Oldsmobile, we glimpse the first word of *Goodbye Columbus* (1969) displayed on a cinema hoarding behind him.

5. *Evening Chronicle*, 22 July 1970. *Carter's the Name*, scenes 14, 16, 18, 20.

6. The pre-production script includes a longer telephone conversation that supplies information about Margaret's marriage to a seaman (*Carter's the Name*, scenes 19 and 21).

7. Hodges, personal communication with the author, 7 May 2002.

8. Newcastle-upon-Tyne *Journal*, 8 September 1970.

9. www.mbspecial.worldonline.co.uk/getcarter/extras/longbar2.htm

10. *Carter's the Name*, scenes 23 and 24.

11. DVD commentary.

12. Michael Caine, DVD commentary.

13. A similar fantasy of Stateside on Tyneside would be evoked in *Stormy Monday* (Mike Figgis, 1988).

14. The shooting script contains a deadpan moment in which the dignity of the undertaker is punctured by a sly fart in the hearse (*Carter's the Name*, scene 37).

15. www.mbspecial.worldonline.co.uk/getcarter/afterfuneral.htm

16. *Carter's the Name*, scenes 55–9.

17. Ibid., scenes 60–67.

18. DVD commentary.

19. Lewis and Hughman, *Most Unnatural*, pp. 45–7.

20. *Journal*, 22 August 1970. The house was built in 1872 as a summer residence for a wealthy banking family in Darlington. Local memories suggest that during Landa's ownership it was visited by the Krays and its grounds patrolled by armed guards. Sold soon after filming to an acquaintance of Landa, Dryderdale was almost gutted in a suspicious fire. It was eventually restored as a family home and guesthouse in 1992.

21. DVD commentary.

22. *Carter's the Name*, scene 95.

23. Lewis and Hughman, *Most Unnatural*, pp. 36–8.

24. www.mdspecial.worldonline.co.uk/getcarter/pinklane.htm

25. Hodges quoted in Hodgkinson, 'The Making of *Get Carter*', p. 61.

26. Britt Ekland, *True Britt*, New York: Berkley, 1982, p. 128.

27. DVD commentary.

28. Hall, *Raising Caine*, p. 172.

29. Hodgkinson, 'The Making of *Get Carter*', p. 58.

30. *Journal*, 8 September 1970.

31. *Carter's the Name*, scene 112.

32. www.mbspecial.worldonline.co.uk/getcarter/extras.htm

33. Catterall and Wells, *Your Face Here*, p. 92.

34. Lewis, *Jack's Return Home*, p. 110.

35. Ibid., p. 64.

36. 'A little party for the offspring while Mummy and Daddy kissed the Chief Inspector's bum', as Lewis described it (*Jack's Return Home*, p. 104).

37. DVD commentary.

38. A northern marching band subsequently featured in *East is East* (Damien O'Donnell, 2000), a film set in the year of *Get Carter*'s release, 1971.

39. Vincent Landa was the owner of a red E-type Jaguar that had been borrowed by his brother and Dennis Stafford on the night of Sibbet's murder. Sibbet's body was discovered in his Mark X Jaguar.

40. Shakespeare, *Hamlet*, III.iv.204.

41. Carter's arrival by car was hastily filmed after a linking sequence in which he abandoned his car to shake off Peter's pursuing Jaguar was dropped.

42. The relevant movement order for the production unit reveals that the location used for this scene was the about-to-be-demolished Wentworth Place (now Gloucester Terrace) in Newcastle's West End.

43. Although Valadimir Propp's *Morphology of the Folktale* (2nd edn, Austin: University of Texas, 1968) had been in English translation for a decade before Lewis came to write his novel, its ideas were not really adopted by film studies until the 1970s.

44. DVD commentary.

45. Hodges' DVD commentary. The top of the Gateshead car park was used again as a location for the opening scene of the Newcastle-set *Purely Belter* (Mark Herman, 2000).

46. The flats, which remain standing today, originally formed part of a 1960s development called St Cuthbert's Village, near the banks of the Tyne in west Gateshead.

47. Caine, DVD commentary.

48. Hodges, ibid.

49. Ibid.

50. Locations were changed after the production unit arrived in Newcastle. Carter was originally to seek out Albert (twice) in his caravan before murdering him at the allotment where he kept his pigeons (*Carter's the Name*, scenes 155–61).

51. Hodges, 'NFT Discussion', p. 120.

52. Hodges, DVD commentary.

53. *Carter's the Name*, scene 161.

54. DVD commentary.

55. On the role of blind men in *Brighton Rock* see Steve Chibnall, 'Purgatory at the End of the Pier: Imprinting a Sense of Place Through *Brighton Rock*', in Alan Burton et al., *The Family Way: The Boulting Brothers and British Film Culture*, Trowbridge: Flicks, 2000, pp. 134–42.

56. *Get Carter. The Screenplay*, London: Sight and Sound, 1999, p. 34.

57. Ibid., p. 49.

58. Hodges, DVD commentary.

59. Ibid.

60. *Carter's the Name*, scenes 162–72.

61. The last line is a quotation from Seneca's *Agamemnon*, I.154.

62. DVD commentary.

63. www.mbspecial.worldonline.co.uk/getcarter/extras/hodges.htm

64. *Carter's the Name*, scene 177.

65. The sub-post office is open curiously late on a Saturday. In Lewis's novel, Carter persuades the proprietor to open after hours.

66. DVD commentary.

67. The sequence was filmed at Hardwick Hall Park near Blackhall Colliery.

68. DVD commentary.

69. The lifestyles of professional seacoalers are depicted in the Amber Films docu-drama *Seacoal* (1985).

70. DVD commentary.

71. www.mbspecial.worldonline.co.uk/getcarter/extras/130lds.htm

72. Thomas Middleton or Cyril Tourneur, *The Revenger's Tragedy*, V.iii.119.

73. DVD commentary.
74. Ibid.
75. Ibid.
76. Dollimore, *Radical Tragedy*, p. 60–61.

3. DEATH AND RESURRECTION

1. The poster also includes an image of a woman struggling with a male assailant that seems to belong to another film.
2. *Kinematograph Weekly*, 6 March 1971.
3. *Evening News*, 11 March 1971. Rather against the critical grain, Nigel Andrews in the *Monthly Film Bulletin* (April 1971) argued that *Get Carter*'s 'picturesque violence' was unable to redeem its 'perfunctory plot, its mechanical manipulation of characters or a vision of the British underworld that relies totally on cliché'. Nobody but Caine, he complained, was allowed to develop their characters.
4. *Observer*, 14 March 1971.
5. *Daily Telegraph*, 12 March 1971.
6. *Sunday Telegraph*, 14 March 1971. See also *Photoplay*, April 1971; Christopher Hudson in the *Spectator*, 20 March 1971; David Gillard in the *Daily Sketch*, Cecil Wilson in the *Daily Mail* and Alexander Walker in the *Evening Standard* (all 11 March 1971).
7. *The Times*, 12 March 1971.
8. *Daily Express*, 10 March 1971.
9. *Sunday Express*, 14 March 1971; *Sun*, 11 March 1971; *Sunday People*, 14 March 1971.
10. *Daily Mail*, 11 March 1971.
11. *Daily Mirror*, 11 March 1971.
12. *Loaded*, 58, February 1999.
13. Caine quoted in Hall, *Raising Caine*, p. 169.
14. *Kinematograph Weekly*, 1 May 1971.
15. *Kinematograph Weekly*, 15 May 1971.
16. *Kinematograph Weekly*, 5 June 1971.
17. *Empire*, December 2000.
18. *Variety*, 20 January 1971. The review praised the 'outstanding photography', 'terrific editing' and 'excellent' cast, as well as the contributions of Roy Budd and the film's designers, and the talent demonstrated by Mike Hodges. *Variety* was particularly impressed by the 'good taste' shown by the film and the 'genuinely artistic way in which the genre is handled'.
19. *The Village Voice*, 18 March 1971.
20. *Time*, 22 March 1971.
21. Brother of producer/director Roger.
22. This is evident from numerous plot details and treatments, not least the film's ending on a rocky beach with a sniper.
23. To be fair, Shag does his best to point out the double standards at work when, finally cornered by Tackett, he calls him 'an animal' and asks: 'What are you killing me for? How many sixteen-year-olds have you pulled for the Bix brothers? They have fathers and brothers too.'

24. *Monogram*, 3, 1972.

25. Alexander Walker, *National Heroes*, London: Harrap, 1985.

26. *Film Dope*, 25, November 1982.

27. Patrick Wright, *On Living in an Old Country: The National Past in Contemporary Britain*, London: Verso, 1985, p. 2.

28. Bruce Kaywin, 'After Midnight', in J. P. Telotte (ed.), *The Cult Film Experience*, pp. 18–25.

29. Wright, *On Living* …, p. 5.

30. www.mbspecial.worldonline.co.uk/getcarter/me.htm

31. *The Prisoner* was a 1960s television series with a sense of mystery and entrapment similar to Hodges' film.

32. Amy Redpath, 'Film Portrayals of the North East of England', BA dissertation, Faculty of Humanities, De Montfort University (unpublished), 2002.

33. Ibid.

34. *Empire*, December 1993 and January 1994.

35. Murphy, 'A Revenger's Tragedy', p. 129.

36. Umberto Eco, '*Casablanca*: Cult Movies and Intertextual Collage', *SubStance*, 47, 1985, pp. 3–12. Michael Brady, the Newcastle man who dedicated most of his spare time over two years to tracking down and photographing the locations used in *Get Carter* for his Web site, did not see the film until its video release.

37. Gidney, *Street Life*, p. 128.

38. Mick Eaton, 'Fog and Drizzle', *Sight and Sound*, August 1993.

39. Quoted in George K. Hunter (ed.), Introduction to *The Malcontent*, London: Methuen, 1975, p. xx.

40. Tim Southwell, *Getting Away with It: The Inside Story of Loaded*, London: Random House, 1998, p. 17.

41. Southwell, *Getting Away with It*, p. 61.

42. *Loaded*, 20, December 1995.

43. *Arena*, 12, 1988.

44. *Loaded*, 58, February 1999. Anecdotal evidence of the growth of *Get Carter*'s popularity among a new constituency of viewers in the mid-1990s is provided by Ted Lewis's widow, Jo Whittle. In 1997 she told Paul Duncan: 'I'm staggered by the number of young people I've met who think *Get Carter* is absolutely superb. At the time, Ted and I thought that, but we didn't get the impression that everyone else did as well. It didn't have that kind of impact' (Duncan, 'All the Way Home').

45. *Neon*, May 1997.

46. *Neon*, September 1997.

47. *Empire*, September 1997.

48. *Crime Time*, 9, 1997. *Carter* also made the cover of *Classic Television*, April/ May 1998.

49. www.us.imdb.com/Ratings?0067128

50. www.us.imdb.com/CommentsShow?0067128

51. *Independent*, 4 June 1999.

52. *Independent on Sunday*, 13 June 1999.

53. Ibid.

54. *Morning Star*, 12 March 1971.

55. Other female reviewers seemed less concerned about *Carter*'s sexual politics. Dilys Powell admired Caine's 'insolently cool, callously lethal' performance (*Sunday Times*, 14 March 1971), while the brief review by Madeline Harmsworth in the *Sunday Mirror* (14 March 1971) praised the film as a 'top-quality thriller'.

56. Redpath, 'Film Portrayals'.

57. www.us.imdb.com/Ratings/0067128. Given that only fifty-three women had registered a vote, however, we should be cautious in drawing conclusions from these data.

58. Staiger, 'The Politics of Film Canons'.

59. BFI Press Information, June 1999.

60. *Sunday Times*, 25 April 1999.

61. *The Times*, 5 June 1999.

62. Ibid.

63. *Guardian*, 28 May 1999.

64. *Guardian*, 13 June 1999.

65. *The Times*, 10 June 1999.

66. *Evening Standard*, 10 June 1999.

67. This box-office gross made *Carter* the thirteenth most successful British film of the forty-two released that year (excluding co-productions) (bfi.org.uk/facts/stats/1999/ukfeatures).

68. The genre had already received belated academic recognition with the publication of Chibnall and Murphy's *British Crime Cinema*, which included two pieces on *Carter* and the film's poster image on its cover.

69. Ed Barnett, 'The Guide: British Gangsters', *Esquire*, February 2000, pp. 114–23.

70. 'Focus: *Get Carter*', ibid., pp. 50–58.

71. Elizabeth Weitzman teased visitors to the website Film.com with descriptions of one of 'the best films you've never seen' ('Every shot is composed with extraordinary judgement; each detail is finer than the last … ').

72. As part of its project of reconstitution, Kay's film scrambles the characters of Kinnear and Brumby, and collapses together the characters of Margaret and Glenda.

73. *Evening Standard*, 3 October 2000.

74. *Total Film*, November 2000. *Hotdog*, December 2000, p. 110.

75. Hodgkinson, 'The Making of *Get Carter*', pp. 54–61.

76. Clark Collis, 'Number One Gangster', *Empire*, December 2000, pp. 124–30.

77. Endorsements from *Uncut* and *Total Film* used in the advertising of the video.

78. *Hotdog*, February 2001, pp. 42–55.

79. '*Venit in nostras tandem vindicta, venit et tota quidem.*'

80. *Empire*, December 2000.

81. DVD commentary.

82. See, for example, Barbara Klinger, 'Digressions at the Cinema: Reception and Mass Culture', *Cinema Journal*, 28 (4), 1989, pp. 3–26; Thomas Schatz, 'The New Hollywood', in Jim Collins et al. (eds), *Film Theory Goes to the Movies*, London: Routledge, 1993, pp. 8–36.

83. *New Statesman*, 29 August 1997.

84. *Evening Standard*, 10 June 1999.

Select Bibliography

Adams, Mark, *Mike Hodges*, Harpenden: Pocket Essentials, 2001.

Barnett, Ed, 'The Guide: British Gangsters', *Esquire*, February 2000, pp. 114–23.

Billson, Anne, *My Name is Michael Caine*, London: Muller, 1991.

Caine, Michael, *What's It All About*, London: Arrow, 1993.

Catterall, Ali and Simon Wells, *Your Face Here: British Cult Movies Since the Sixties*, London: Fourth Estate, 2001.

Chibnall, Steve and Robert Murphy (eds), *British Crime Cinema*, London: Routledge, 1999.

Collis, Clark, 'Number One Gangster', *Empire*, December 2000, pp. 124–30.

Darke, Chris, 'From Gangland to the Casino Table', *Independent*, 4 June 1999.

Davies, Steven Paul, *Get Carter and Beyond: The Cinema of Mike Hodges*, London: Batsford, 2002.

Dewe Mathews, Tom, 'Now Get the Son of *Get Carter*', *Evening Standard*, 11 June 1999, pp. 34–5.

Duncan, Paul, 'All the Way Home: Ted Lewis', *Crime Time*, 9, 1997, pp. 22–5.

'Focus: *Get Carter*', *Esquire*, February 2000, pp. 50–58.

Freedland, Michael, *Michael Caine*, London: Orion, 2000.

Gallagher, Elaine, *Candidly Caine*, London: Pan Books, 1991.

Gidney, Chris, *Street Life: The Bryan Mosley Story*, London: HarperCollins, 1999.

Hall, William, *Raising Caine*, London: Sidgwick and Jackson, 1981.

Hodges, Mike, *Carter's the Name*, revised version, 30 June 1970, Eye: ScreenPress, 2001.

— *Get Carter: A Screenplay*, Eye: ScreenPress, 2001.

— 'Getting Carter … ', *Crime Time*, 9, 1997, pp. 20–21.

Hodgkinson, Mike, 'The Making of *Get Carter*', *Later*, 19, December 2000, p. 57.

Hutchings, Peter, 'When the Going Gets Tough', in T. Faulkner (ed.), *Northumbrian Panorama: Studies in the History and Culture of the North East of England*, London: Octavian Press, 1996.

Lewis, David and Peter Hughman, *Most Unnatural: An Inquiry into the Stafford Case*, Harmondsworth: Penguin, 1971.

Lewis, Ted, *Jack's Return Home*, retitled *Carter*, London: Pan Books, 1970.

Spencer, Neil, 'The Caine Mutiny', *Uncut*, June 1998, pp. 31–3.

Walker, Alexander, *National Heroes*, London: Harrap, 1986.

www.mbspecial.worldonline.co.uk/getcarter/

www.btinternet.com/~ms.dear